"If you're not familiar with tʰ
to catch up with some of thɛ
showcases the creative talentʂ
to their own distinct rhythm
performed aloud, their transiʈ
entry captures a raw essenc
That's the power of words."
—Denvil Saine, *HX Magazine*

"When spoken word became
and aspiring bohemians, a friɡ
poetry focused not on honestʏ
took center stage. *Bullets &*
honesty to the genre with iʈs poignant poems, which touch upon
subjects such as love, identity, ruptured families, revolution, death,
rejection, and bigotry. Although not all of the poems dazzle, there are no
space-fillers here. Emmanuel Xavier hits high notes with "A Simple
Poem" and "Legendary," but it's Travis Montez and Staceyann Chin
who steal the show with their viscerally visual accounts."
—Celia San Miguel, *New York Post*

"Round out your queer canon with a couple of cannonballs fired straight
from the militant front lines of urban spoken word expression. All the
poets you know (or will soon enough) are anthologized in this potent
collection. Led by Puerto Rican wordsmith Emanuel Xavier, the rough
riders of the new poetic frontier are blazing in their saddles here, spittin'
the kind of politically charged fire-tempered-with-humor that makes us
love these bad boys so."
—*Next Magazine*

"The poets in *Bullets & Butterflies* vary in terms of style and talent, but all
celebrate what it is to be queer and outspoken in today's world. For
those familiar with the slam poetry scene in New York and San
Francisco, this anthology is a chance to see on page poems that they
heretofore have only heard over steaming mugs of coffee. For those new
to queer spoken word poetry, this anthology is a window into a world
where having a big mouth and plenty to say is an asset rather than a
liability."
—Winnie McCroy, *Edge Boston*

"All the poems in this anthology, in some way or other, are complexly
entangled when it comes to writing about what it is to be American and
queer. And what I admire most about the anthology is that the form—
that is, the spoken word form—offers a space in which these poets can
share their experiences with readers in a way that isn't alienating, that
may leave the reader clamoring for the nearest microphone, waiting for
these potent words to explode the air."
—D. Antwan Stewart, *Lambda Book Report*

Bullets &
Butterflies:
queer spoken word poetry

edited by
Emanuel Xavier

suspect thoughts press
www.suspectthoughtspress.com

Cover design by Shane Luitjens/Torquere Creative
Book design by Greg Wharton/Suspect Thoughts Press

First Edition: February 2005
10 9 8 7 6 5 4 3 2

Library of Congress Cataloging-in-Publication Data

Bullets & butterflies : queer spoken word poetry / edited by Emanuel Xavier.
    p. cm.
  ISBN 0-9746388-5-4 (pbk.)
  1. Gays' writings, American. 2. American poetry--21st century. 3. Oral interpretation of poetry. 4. Homosexuality--Poetry. I. Title: Bullets and butterflies.

PS591.G38B85 2005
811'.6080920664--dc22

                                        2004030969

Suspect Thoughts Press
2215-R Market Street, #544
San Francisco, CA 94114-1612
www.suspectthoughtspress.com

Suspect Thoughts Press is a terrible infant hell-bent to burn the envelope by publishing dangerous books by contemporary authors and poets exploring provocative social, political, queer, spiritual, and sexual themes.

publication credits

Grateful acknowledgment is made to the following publications in which these poems originally appeared:

Cheryl Boyce-Taylor: "For My Comrades" first appeared in *Raw Air* (Fly By Night Press, 1997). "Plenty Time Pass Fast, Fas Dey So" first appeared in *The World in Us: Lesbian and Gay Poetry of the Next Wave*, Michael Lassell and Elena Georgiou, eds. (St. Martin's Press, 2000).

Regie Cabico: "Gameboy" first appeared in *ALOUD: Voices from the Nuyorican Poets Cafe*, Miguel Algarin and Bob Holman, eds. (Owl Books, 1994).

Daphne Gottlieb: "For Suicide Girls Who Have Considered Extensions/ When Manic Panic Is Enuf" and "Liability" first appeared in *Final Girl* (Soft Skull Press, 2003). "Living Legend" first appeared in *Bottoms Up*, Diana Cage, ed. (Soft Skull Press, 2004).

Marty McConnell: "Homeland" first appeared in *Freedom to Speak*, Scott Woods, ed. (The Wordsmith Press, 2002).

Alix Olson: "America's On Sale" first appeared in *Revolutionary Voices*, Amy Sonnie, ed. (Alyson Books, 2000). "Daughter" and "Warriors" first appeared in *Burning Down the House* (Soft Skull Press, 2000). "Dorothea Tanning" first appeared in *Seattle Journal for Social Justice*, Fall/Winter 2004.

Shailja Patel: "Dreaming in Gujurati" first appeared in *Sows Ear Poetry Review*, Summer 2001. "This Is How It Feels" first appeared in *From Porn to Poetry*, Susannah Indigo, ed. (Samba Mountain Press, 2001). "Eater of Death" first appeared in *What If? A Journal of Radical Possibilities*, Winter 2002.

Emanuel Xavier: "Outside" and "A Simple Poem" first appeared in *Queer Codex: Chile Love*, Winter 2004. "Legendary" first appeared in *Coloring Book: An Eclectic Anthology of Fiction & Poetry by Multicultural Writers*, Boice-Terrel Allen, ed. (Rattlecat Press, 2004).

contents

"We must learn words can be bullets or butterflies,
we must learn to say what we mean and mean what we say."

—Piri Thomas
from the Afterword to the 30th Anniversary Edition of *Down These
Mean Streets*

foreword

President Bush came out.

(In favor of a Constitutional amendment banning gay marriage, that is!) (Do not forget: the last change in the marriage statutes was to allow lovers from different races to marry.)

Not homosexual rights, but homo sapiens' rights. Not the rights of women or men, not yellows, whites, browns, blacks, not shorts or talls, text or performance, but the inherent dignity of humanity *in toto* (especially when in drag!).

It's in the language, these delightful ambiguities, as it's in our bodies, and the poets in this wonderful, luscious, vibrant, wicked, wise anthology know all about it. It's what they do—accept the variousness of the body (the armpit, Allen Ginsberg reminds us after all, is holy) and the elasticity of language to forge an identity in art that's at once sensuous, socially conscious, savvy, and seriously pissed off.

Gays have always been in the forefront of U.S. poetry: Whitman, Stein, Hughes, Ginsberg. But it's at this curious hinge of twenty-first-century NOW that poetry itself has found its way into the ear of public consciousness, so that we are finally hearing Whitman's varied carols tambourining. Orality is reemerging in poetry; so it's natural that gays are writing and performing some terrific poems.

Herein Emanuel Xavier blends the performing poetry scene round these states with the drag balls and queer Houses in New York. The poets in this anthology are not generally known outside the Slam, Performance, and Hip Hop Poetry worlds, and certainly it's been difficult to find their work on the page anywhere. But here they are at last, spinning on dialectics political, genderfied, aesthetic.

Now that they're on the page in front of you, get busy, critics, and deconstruct these wails of beauty!

Now that they're harnessed to the page, you can see the care and craft, the rehearsed spontaneity, that goes into creating what Walter Ong calls "voicings." It's the old bugaboo—"does it work on the page?" The taut internal rhymes of Celena Glenn. The long-lined narratives of Horehound Stillpoint. The look of the dub Creole of Cheryl Boyce-Taylor. The open field of Maurice Jamal. The look and textual sophistication of these poems belie any other definition. And besides: these are poems that mutate to sound before your ears, as good a trick as writing can do. These poems invite you in. They ask you if you want to dance. After that, it's up to you.

So let this stand as the Foreword to *Bullets & Butterflies: queer spoken word poetry*. Let it be known that I am for words, that these poems are made out of words, and that there are purposes for books that a slam, reading, performance, concert cannot accomplish. These poems can be traveled with, assigned for class, read wherever you like. You can study them for intricacies, for sound-meaning syntheses.

And since all these poets are united in a single tome, you can sleep with them all in a single night, whether gay or straight, no difference.

And I recommend this course. Because the worlds that these poets dare dream are the futures that require poetry to be foreseen.

—Bob Holman
New York City, 2005

introduction

The microphone stands alone in the spotlight. The crowd is loud and lively, waiting for your voice to silence them with poetry, for the echoes of your soul to bounce off the politics of war, the longing for love, the need for acceptance.

Sometimes words assault the audience from the stage like bullets, wounding quick and deeply. Sometimes poems leave lips like butterflies, beautifully decorating the room with hope.

Spoken word poetry has both been greatly criticized and widely celebrated.

As spoken word artists, we have little interest in pretending to come across as academics. Many of us have developed our crafts on the streets or in underground cafes or stumbled upon poetry by sheer accident. This does not mean, however, that we are ignorant of the gifts of William Shakespeare and Sylvia Plath and Langston Hughes.

We do not write simply for the applause of an audience but for the belief that poetry, like all art, is not just for the elite. It is something to be shared and appreciated by everyone, regardless of age, education, class, sexual preference.

Much like our queer community, spoken word poetry has often been considered taboo and out of the mainstream, even though it has contributed significantly to culture. Much like Hip Hop, it is still thought of as controversial and dangerous, despite its undeniable enthusiasm and influence. Of course, this very rebelliousness is the reason spoken word poetry has enjoyed a lot of attention and success.

Queer voices have been at the vanguard of the spoken word rebellion, from the very beginning, vibrantly cascading beyond sexuality and into the political. Though everyone included in this collection identifies as *queer*, we are all concerned with so much more than just expressing our desire. Audre Lorde, a spiritual presence throughout this collection, once said, "In the forefront of our move toward change, there is only poetry to hint at possibility made real."

But it is our brothers and sisters who are out on the streets protesting for peace and fighting for our rights who are the true inspiration for this collection. Words spoken cannot create change, but they can motivate and influence beyond sexual boundaries. Poetry can bridge the differences and highlight the similarities.

This book was originally meant to include many more spoken word artists that have emerged from the queer community. And though there may not have been enough room for every poem to fit here, there are voices out there that deserve to be heard. And more will come. For whether it is through publishing, recordings, television, film, theater, or visual art collaborations, we will continue to contribute creatively because one of the greatest attributes of being *queer* is our passion. As Keith Haring said, "To find hope and beauty in the face of struggle and oppression is certainly a challenge but also carries with it the greatest rewards."

On behalf of each of the spoken word artists featured in this collection, thank you for reading these poems without our actual voices or physical movements taking center stage in a crowded venue dimly lit with candles and decorated with fresh flowers, haunting percussions perhaps playing in the background.

After all, spoken word starts off with the solitary act of writing a poem, and with that said, this book is dedicated to all those who ever felt they were alone.

—Emanuel Xavier

Rink Foto

horehound stillpoint

Gregory Richard Taylor, a.k.a Horehound Stillpoint, born in 1952 and raised in Columbus, Ohio, wanted to be a writer ever since he heard the name Dostoyevsky fall from the lips of a high school English teacher. His teenage poetry danced — with two left feet — into print in the school's annual periodical as early as 1967.

Working hard enough to get straight *A*s, he graduated valedictorian in a class of seven hundred just so he could give a speech to the assembled masses. In spite of that roaring success, it would be twenty-one years before he would again read his writing in front of an audience (proving, perhaps, that Greg wasn't terribly bright after all).

A few failed romances later, and after coming out to friends and family, and with a list of tricks much, much longer than his arm, Greg quit Columbus for California, where he hitchhiked up and down the coast, Mendocino to San Luis Obispo.

Returning routinely to San Francisco — where he stayed in what was then called a Gay Mission — he ended up meeting a man, Michael Ventura, who was an honest-to-god hippie, and artist, weight lifter, and DJ. They eloped, like outlaws in the night, to the woods of the Russian River. Their honeymoon consisted of three months in a cabin without electricity or running water. Greg was trying to get in touch with Whitman's transcendent grasses, while Michael built fires, cooked, played Zappa and Cream on a kid's stereo hooked up to a car battery, and provided all the acid two people could eat in one summer on a hippie commune.

In the fifteen years he shared with Michael (in Hawaii, Monterey, Santa Rosa, and mostly San Francisco), Greg wrote two novels and a smattering of short stories, all of which remain happily unpublished. Most of his time and energy was spent being a stoned gay punk rocker and a full-time grouchy waiter.

One day in 1992, Michael, now an ex-lover and best friend, called to say he wanted to kill himself. In the subsequent flood of anger, frustration, guilt, fear, disbelief, and hope, nine poems bubbled up and spilled out onto the page, and the voice that would be Horehound's was born. Three of the poems were read later that evening, in a South of Market coffee shop, comfortably near the hard-core leather bars of San Francisco. A dirty, scruffy, biker-looking dude reacted with the most encouraging words: "Good shit, man." One of those first poems later appeared in the anthology *Gents, Bad Boys, and Barbarians*.

In short order, he met the amazing Sparrow 13 Laughingwand, the transcendent Trebor Healey, the brilliant Michelle Tea, and the indescribable Bambi Lake, all regulars at the beloved Paradise Lounge poetry reading, and all queers with tricked-up names.

At this time, a certain Gregg Deborah Taylor (also born Gregory Richard Taylor, but quite a different person altogether) was considered to be the Crown Prince of queer San Francisco, having created Club Chaos, Club Uranus, and Club Screw. The writing Greg Taylor thus took this opportunity to rename himself. Horehound was a favorite candy of his as a child; Stillpoint came from the only poem with which he connected as an adult, from T. S. Eliot's piece about the dance and the still point around which the dance occurs, and how there is no dance without the still point, and there is nothing but the dance...

His early poems were an attempt to translate and transmit the ancient wisdom known as Adwaita Vedanta, which Horehound had been studying, in the *Bhagavad Gita* and the Upanishads, with his guru, Jim Gilman. Sometimes these poems were funny and honest, sometimes pedantic and preachy. A young, straight, innocent-looking girl came up to Horehound after one reading and told him that he was a lot better when he was being "more personal," sharing "that hard-core gay stuff." His words became dirtier and dirtier, instantly and endlessly. In fact, his second self-published chapbook was titled *The Inside Dirt* (the first being *Some Holy Googolplex* and the third, *Dovetail*). One of his scandalous poems, "Reincarnation Woes," was illustrated by KRK Ryden and published by Kapow! Others can be found in the anthologies *Sex Spoken Here, beyond definition, Poetry Nation, Out in the Castro, Poetry Slam, Bend, Don't Shatter*, and *Men, Amplified*.

Horehound quite unwittingly stumbled onto the poetry slam scene, winning the first one he entered without knowing it was going to be a competition. He bombed, big time, in the following semifinals, setting up the operative pattern for his performing career: one step forward, then flat on his face.

Regie Cabico invited him to do readings in New York and Boston, and he also encouraged him to get serious about poetry slams. Horehound eventually made it onto the San Francisco team, going to the nationals in 1996 and 1997. His claim to fame there was topping the list of sexiest male slam poets made by his irrepressible teammates, Tarin Towers and Nancy Depper, in order to piss off the hetero poets who had scored much higher in the actual tournament.

When Michael died, eventually, in a state of dementia full of saints, cute boys, and fiery red horses, Horehound wrote poems. He is writing poems still.

my solution to everything

Promiscuity is my solution to the world's problems.
 Millions of eyes may damn
Me for this: Black road warriors, German shamen,
 Malaysian performance artists
Latino sunworshippers, and the only tent I have big enough
 To bring all these together is my bed.
Lord, make the next one Muslim so I can learn to love what I fear;
 Make him like my father so forgiveness can go deep.
Damn it to hell, I always end up talking about fucking men,
 I only wanted to invoke love.
Truth is I tend to get the two confused.
Truth is single, alone, isolating; I still walk in love I breathe love float

Through love with every muscle every bone nothing but love and I,
 Confused by men, the world, my reactions, and everything
Going to war, playing goddammed games, drowning in a sea
 Of unknowing/knowing
Armageddon doesn't stand a chance against my love.

in the church of the last three minutes, part II

in the church of the last three minutes
my mother will know about every dick I ever had in my mouth
my father will feel every cock I ever had up my butt
we will all know the actual number of sex partners I meant
every time I said ten thousand in one of my poems
my neighbor will know how much I wanted to slap him
ron will know how irritating he was, how much he hurt me
how devastating his betrayal was
gil will know how often I wanted to blow him off the planet
when I worked with him and his hatred night after night
I will know if I really loved michael
or if the actions of my head and heart fell too short of the name
I will know if eric was my great love or my great sickness
I will know if I was as big an asshole to justin as he claimed I was
I will know how jens felt when I told him about having sex
        with someone else the first weekend he spent away from me
my grandmother will see me getting pissed on by that guy
        with the whip
my grandfather will hear me tell spoken word audiences all about it
jesus will know what I wanted to do to stephen king
        and his million-selling novels
        (huh, call that piece of crap a novel?
        I say shove it back up where it came from)
buddha will know how I felt about football players
        making all the money in america just for putting on a jockstrap
mother teresa will see me going into virgin records
        and not giving money to the beggars on the street outside
bob and ted and cary and danny will know I never meant to call them
        trading numbers was just this thing to do after trading blow jobs
all those straight guys in the shower will know
        that I really did want to stick
        my tongue in their assholes, juice 'em up and
        then fuck them blind
my sister will know how foreign I found her life
        marrying for stability, then endless conversations about dinner
audiences will know how much I wanted one man to step
        out of the crowd
        pick me up and carry me off and never put me down again
ah, fuck it, there is no point in keeping anything secret

in the church of the last three minutes of the universe
it will all come out in the wash
you will know my everything
and I will know yours

22 bullets & butterflies

most sorry ass zen idiot

Sitting in the zendo, I can't help but think
I'm sorry I didn't make love the center of my life
Love trumps everything
Before I move into the Zen Center
I need to go on a National Apology Tour
On this planet for fifty years plus, I've been a busy bee
    and a nasty prick
I need to apologize to everyone from Mom to Afghanistan
Special apologies to the men I've fucked and forgotten
    or just didn't call
Also, sorry for the poetry I aired, concerning real people
Who need to get the literal and figurative shit fucked out of them
That ex-boyfriend is not the only one
Who needs to get royally, roughly, religiously fucked
But how often do any of us get what we deserve?
"All the time," my ex-guru used to say
Sorry about the bubbles of low self-esteem
That pop altogether too close to your face
When I move into the Zen Center
I am going to suffer like a son of a bitch
Take refuge in that
I want to be able to sit without resentment, without regret
For the peace and well-being of the planet
For the liberation of all sentient beings
For happiness, for freedom from suffering, for nonattachment
    to misery
For knowledge, wisdom, and Attainment
For love
Buddhists don't talk much about love
I must be a bad Buddhist indeed
I would give it all up for love
Zen priests tell me to sit down, shut up, and breathe
I may be a sorry ass idiot, but when I move into the Zen Center
I am going to be more zen than the Art of Motorcycle Maintenance
I'm going to be more zen than whoever came up with *whatever*
I'm gonna be more zen than Yoda, Spock, and Galadriel put together
If I see the Buddha on my walks through the zen garden
I will tell him to shut up, roll over, and breathe
You've been God long enough
Now let me be the daddy
I guess I should resurrect my father so I can tell him how sorry I am

For confusing him with God
For thinking everything in the world was his fault
I'm sorry to the whole world for being so obsessed with men
When I move into the Zen Center
I am asking for a female roommate
She better be really feminine too
If they put me in with a butch dyke
With shoulders for days
Severe titties and a boychick ass
I could end up forgetting about the whole dick thing
Plunge myself into a brand-new sorry mess
Please, God, even though You don't exist in the zendo
Don't make me be bi at this late stage of my life
Aren't I confused enough?
When I move into the Zen Center
I hope I can go six months without sex
I hope my head doesn't explode
I hope my knees don't fall off
I hope my prostate doesn't get cancerously cranky
I hope the God who doesn't exist there
Sends me the perfect roommate
        (someone I won't want to kill after two weeks)
Might as well take him on my National Apology Tour right now
I'm sorry I'm this gaseous
I'm sorry I'm so timid and scared and accusingly silent
        and arrogantly withdrawn
I'm sorry I'm not that funny in real life
When I move into the Zen Center, I will think of more things
        to apologize for
I'll weave a brand-new worldwide web of apology
Till there's nothing left but one man standing
Or sitting, as the case may be...sitting...quietly, utterly still
Nothing left but love
What else but
Love trumpets the world into being and love blows it all away
It's too much to ask for and yet I ask
When I move into the Zen Center
Can I be brand-new?
When I move into the Zen Center
Can apologies be things of the past?
When I move into the Zen Center
If the center isn't love...can someone take me out to the edge and back?
I feel as if I'm almost there and somehow already coming
I'm still coming, I am

Don't stop now, you fuckin' idiot
That's all love is, you know: not stopping

all the world's a badboy beach

I know what planet I'm on, when I go to Badboy Beach
Heaven, envisioned by a baby fag. Smell: this is
Where I come from, where I begin again
Feel the earth growing, breathing, disintegrating. Nine eleven, 2001

And every nine eleven since, I come to Badboy Beach,
     though the Golden Gate
Bridge gleams target-like between San Francisco and the rest
     of the world.
You can't kill me here. Not with my feet in sand and tide
Nor these voluptuous women, smiling about cream-centered
     secrets of life

Nor mostly naked men: touching, touchable, touched
On a planet where queerness runs like veins through clay and iron ore.
You can't kill me. If you blast my shadow on the cliff, I become water;
If you send tsunamis, I slip into a crack. Kissing my man here

We melt, smile, becoming our veins, remember — oh, I remember
     and radiate
An ancient revolution called love.

bottom who doesn't

I fell in love this week
Well, in...*and* out, but still
It's rare for me to find myself in this position
Because I am a hard man to fit
Being a ninety percent clean and sober poet
(The ten percent is the one beer I allow myself
Twice a month just to cut through the terror)
(Plus, a half a hit of acid now and then
So I can go see the Buzzcocks
And the Cramps, on consecutive nights
In spite of my outrageously advanced age)
Nothing about me is pure or simple
I'm a bottom who doesn't like to get fucked
I'm a top who doesn't like to take control
I'm a man from Venus with female Mars rising
I'm a spiritual sex addict
I'm a romantic who turns into hot stuff at orgies
I'm a Blow Buddies regular and you wouldn't think
After all these years and men and lessons
That I would still be ready to pick out china patterns
After spending ninety minutes with a man
But I am...I am
A butch motherfucker with a twelve-year-old girl at my inner core
I'm a huge sissy and one of the original punk rockers
I'm a motormouth with social anxiety disorder
I'm a control freak who loves to surrender
I'm a perfectionist who can't get organized
I don't ask anymore, "Where is my tribe?"
There is no tribe
There is no tight-knit group of loving friends à la *Queer as Folk*
So when a man comes along
Who's into playing in the bushes, who's into sunsets at the beach
Who shows interest in the world of poetry
Who isn't a drunk and isn't a drug addict
Who calls me back when I call him
(We're down to less than point one percent of the gay male population
    of SF by now)
Who likes to be on top even when he's being a bottom
Who not only sees my male and female facets
But who is willing to let me see his and hers
Who can take a break in the lovemaking and have some silly laughs

And still be turned on a moment later
Then I'm starting to fall in love
Even though he is twenty years younger than me
And I know that's a problem
Even though he doesn't even live on this continent
And I know that's a setup for heartbreak
Even though he is much too beautiful and well built for me
And I know that's going to be a challenge
Then I take the week that I'm given
And I say thank you
I take the sleepless nights when the bed suddenly feels so empty
And I say Okay
I take the night, or two, of tears
And I say Hallelujah
Maybe there's life in this old girl yet
I am an ancient rock 'n' roller who still believes
I would have gone to France for Alain
I thought he was the greatest thing since sliced brie
His smile is like the sun appearing from behind one of those damn Alps
His cock is the perfect halfway mark between a cream puff
    and a nice big salami
His body has more curves than the Tour de France
It would have been great to travel that course year after year
I would have followed him to the moon in a parallel universe
In this one...I'm a vagabond who never goes anywhere
I'm a dreamer with both feet on the ground
I'm the Boy Named Sue, a Ball of Confusion, the Acid Queen,
    and Aladdin Sane
And I don't think I'm any different from anybody else

confessions of a jerk-off retard

My first orgasm was with a friend
He called it milking the cow
One hand tickled   while   the other went to work
We were what would now be called: goal-oriented
Our eyes glazed and intense as revolutionaries
It would have been romantic if everything had been different
Me being the latchkey kid, he came over Monday through Friday
We had our routine, terrifying and necessary
        and transcendent as milking a cow could be
One day I decided to try it on my own
I pumped, jerked and was pulling my milker
        when the door sounds of mother interrupted my experiment
I stuffed my overloaded cow-cucumber-slug thingie
        back into my tight teenage pants
Cramped and practically tied into knots it remained
        during dinner and tv and questions about homework
When finally, time for bed, ready for pajamas
I looked and saw my misshapen, creased, bent, mushroomed monster
        and I thought I broke my dick
I broke my dick
That moment I made a deal with God
I will never touch my dick like that again
If it gets better after this time
I will never beat off again
Omigawd, I broke my dick
I can never do that again
I will only let other boys do it for me
That was the deal
This is a tool that other boys know what to do with
Not me, not me
This is a toy that other boys know how to play with
In the library, in the swimming pool, in the bathroom at the
        mall, in the department store during christmas shopping,
        in the back of the bus, out by the railroad tracks in June,
        down in the parking garage, in your car, in your apartment
Take your teeth out I don't care
5'6," 240, Vangelis on the stereo, sure, go ahead
You wanna touch it, touch it
It's yours, this body
It looks like mine but it's not, it's yours
Then, when I ended up in a podunk college

without queer bars or lonely old men in bus depots
or horny gay guys in libraries
(Trust me, it was straight as astronomy)
I went three months with no touch, nobody and nothing
Too uptight even for wet dreams
I thought I would go mad unless I took matters in hand
I took a pencil
Finally, yes, I took a pencil
And without even undoing my pants
I poked at my jeans
I poked and prodded for a full 30 seconds...with a number 2 pencil
Okay, the eraser end
I prodded my pecker with a pencil eraser
Being the jerk-off retard that I am
I came...in less than a minute
After which, I checked my underwear
And there, along with a half pint of cum
In my midwestern tidy whites
Were spots of blood
Where there should have been just cum
There was blood
Omigawd, I broke it again
I broke my dick
God, oh God, I forgot the deal
Wait, can't we go back
If you put it back the way it was
I'll put it back where it was
Which I did and — Lo and Behold — the next day
There was no blood: so I packed my bags
and moved to the big city with all the queer boys
and horny old men and hot tricks and married bisexual guys
and gay bars and dark alleys and bushes at the beach
and beating off became entirely unnecessary
So now you know one story of how someone can become
the kind of Freak *you can't take home to mother*
But it's all right: this world has many such stories
We might as well all get comfortable

it came from behind

I haven't gotten fucked for fifteen years
But 2004 is up for grabs
Here I am: ankles up around Jimmy's ears
He said he was a talented top and he was right
Here I am: "Ow! Wait. Unhhh. Slow. Down. Okay. Owwww!"
Unsure if this counts as taking it like a man
Here I am: breathing through the pain
Make it hard, make it hurt, why not
I had to swallow my outrage and disgust
At seeing pictures of those Iraqi prisoners getting tortured
There I was, thinking the human race might be getting better
Wiser, gentler, more loving, more compassionate
Man—Jimmy!—do I ever need to get fucked
I wanted to leap from the Golden Gate Bridge
Make a sign with one of those awful pictures of pain and humiliation
Scribble *Not in My World*
And just jump
Thing is, the Official Incorporated Religion of Greedy Power Mongers
Already blames fags, dykes, and trannies for what happened
     in Abu Graib
We dragged America the Formerly Beautiful
Through leather fairs, S & M, Pride celebrations, male pulchritude
Parades of shamelessly powerful female breasts and gender jumble
Now we're going to ruin marriage
Now we're coming after the children
Now we're infiltrating armies
Dedicating it all to the Burning of the Bush
Might as well call it a religious experience
Up to my eyeballs in blood and bile, piss and spunk
Wicked thick bottled-up rage
It's gonna take a corkscrew dick to straighten out my shit
Yeah, I got fucked last night for the first time since 1989
We did fuck safe though—we will fuck safe too
Precisely because so many *real* assholes want us dead
'Cause the world is different I have to be different
I have to let it all inside
I want to be a gaping hole
My wound as big as all outdoors
I wanna be fucked alive by the army I believe in: Volunteer
Busting out of their briefs, fully loaded, and—you know—*consenting*
The future, this country, and my ass

Fucked, fucked, fucked
Thank you, Presidential Prick
Thing is, heroes and villains can be hard to distinguish
They both come from behind
Lighting a mortal fire deep within
Undeniably, irresistibly, unbelievably
I'm alive and so is my ass
Good job, Presidential Prick
You've made me feel Born Again

Seren Divine

celena glenn

Born Celena Renee Glenn in Alabama, by the age of five, she was pounding piano keys for Sunday congregations, enjoying farmside strawberries, and in love with an albino pony named "Princess."

Celena was a military brat, jumping rope on German hilltop army bases and skating at a park located next to a fence which held back the horrors of the holocaust.

In seventh grade, she was commissioned to paint portraits of local "felons." When she presented political campaigns and coloring books constructed of Harriet Tubmans, basketball shoes, and shoulder injuries, her future scholarship propositions were seemingly denied.

Years later, at a Memphis art school, Celena modeled nude for grandmothers, leading a jealous ex to punch the windshield of her Ford (but she got his girl).

While hosting slams at the Nuyorican Poets Cafe, she simultaneously managed to win two National Poetry Slam Championships with team Urbana and was crowned the first Individual Champion at the Bowery Poetry Club.

Celena is currently breast-feeding tomorrow's saints through spoken word education by collaborating, in one way or another, with Urban Word, Teen Speaks, Wingspan Arts, Outward Bound, Lower Eastside Girls Club, Rikers Island Penitentiary, the Whitney Museum, the Studio Museum of Harlem, Russell Simmons, the Knicks, public schools, colleges, brothels, etc.

Her ransom notes have been featured in anthologies and periodicals such as *Spoken Word Revolution, Untold, Time Out, Crush,* and *Serum.* She also dropped a solo album, *Transparent Sand Reflecting the Ego of Crabs,* featuring fully self-produced, recorded, engineered, and ruined electronic, noncategorical, late night confessions of a Jesus complex. Celena is also featured in *Urban Scribe,* a documentary about the lives of contemporary poets.

A ballet-toed bulldozer shoveling blankets off the ice-covered lakes of the heart's malfunctions, Celena Glenn urges that every ghetto, every suburb, every mansion recognize the relativity of circumstance and allow those elements that discriminate, to unify the world as a humanity of oppressed souls.

volcanoes and earthquakes

wrap your chairs in plastic
bundle them up like dreams
because the illustrations of rococo flowers
rendered on cotton
will not grow without air

blame it on the company
conviction is wearing no clothes
and shitting all over the sofa
nauseating love who is upchucking on your mistress
being fucked by your paycheck
because this "fish" called greedy
is on the payroll and looking for a raise

found it in the boss' pants
while looking for a pencil
to erase your name
from the office door you sit behind

why was your name written in graphite
on lined paper
duct-taped to a hardwood door

because you are replaceable
like cheap beer in a can
like the recycled leaves of winter
surpassed by the benjamin leaves of spring
because our kids are well trained in empire takeovers
they know how to hire Mexicans to undercut the price

but don't be upset with your son
he was not yours anyway
cloned from the DNA of Hitler
with a touch of Jay-Z
because your wife left
when you were fired from McDonald's
for not cooking all of the farm animals into the burgers

even
the rats wear Gucci
and steal from the poor

because the rich will bomb the rich to get richer
and leave the remainder to die
in 8ᵗʰ grade project (housings)
that their daughters construct out of Blacks and Latinos

built the traps out of bricks
brought back from Hiroshima as souvenirs

next year
one girl envisions flying to the moon to dig a hole
deep enough to house her outdated Christmas presents
because it is rumored that the 9ᵗʰ grade teachers grade harder

and she is determined to get straight As
and become the first Asshole in the family
to design furniture prepackaged in plastic
with illustrations of deflated balloons
that read "Get Well Soon, America!"

abner louima

we teach our kids to lie
ass up and kiss the dick
of the son of the boss
son of a bitch named Lassie
leashed neck
tied in satin
patterned in blueprints
portraying how to get black and brown thumbprints on the record
enrolling them in the auction
blocks of public housing
of welfare recipients

only the receipts add up to the election
of fifty-some-odd white dicks
no pussies or brown sticks
stuck up the ass of middle America

sitting on toilets
full of capitalistic shit
sucking off green pacifiers
laced with complacency

but not spring shower grass
green like the color of piss on a white wall
after asparagus was served

always with wings

America can kiss my
nose bleeding periodically
into pitchers of Kool-Aid
sipped by children
who get ring around the mouth
clown face rosy at the thought of my contempt

considering how government officials
poison the very food on their own plates
suicidal mad cows
fat pigs in a blanket
embroidered stupid
in wild western font

I type ransom notes to the roaches
that sleep in the corners of my eyes
demanding that they let go of the crumbs

we the people need to let go of crumbs
fuck a slice
bake a loaf
and not in the microwave
use the warmth of heat emitted from your hearts
not some commercialized conviction
programmed to half bake your brains
leaving them sagging in the center
like birthday cakes removed from the oven prematurely

what's for dinner?

the Roach Motel located behind Heaven's Gate
waits for mice and men in hen suits
clucking chickens
fucking Emily Dickinson's
daughter named Hillary "Bush" Clinton

who is next in line
for primetime football
kicking U-Hauls full of servants
of African descendants
rocking pedants of J. Christ
eating fried rice prepared by Mexicans
whose next of kin defended the Alamo
with snow cones and Coke-a-Cola
spitting ebola and salmonella
on the umbrellas of good fellas
in BluBlockers and business suits

who suit Daisy Duke–wearing hoochies
wearing Gucci knockoffs
like colonialists
knocked the Red Socks off of a corn-eating Indian
named Mahatma Gandhi

I bet you my heartbeat
you speak of life like *Loveboat*
but this is a slaveship
get your gun
get your whip
cream on top of tomorrow's jelly-dipped donuts
candy-coated craniums
draining the dumb from boredom
satiated with pacifiers

no green tea will tint my eyes envious
of what is in a man's pocket
or wig
or dirty diaper

shit is shit
no matter what sound it makes when it falls

and love is love
no matter who has the balls
or the Bushes in their White House that turns
and turns into a discotheque
when the children go to bed

these slugs sing us like lullabies
fuck us until we cry
and fry us like the French do to rotten cheese
that swells like our patience
and understanding for communities
who dwell in cells
supposedly homes
that keep them on their knees
and keep them begging please
and keep them on ice
like old meat in the freeze

how sleazy
and how slimy
can a culture be
when believing all that you can be
involves realizing everything you could never
believing that you are better
and free to step on skulls like pebbles
treating people like Fruity Pebbles
just a couple of crumbs in a dish
dismissed like compassion and proportion

if abortion applied to communities
in fetal position with no options
but to starve to death
the breathless souls ruling this country
would dismiss them
like kids in detention
with no intention of ever lending a hand
or a slice of Spam
or ham
or concern

they would burn them like toast
and the urn full of a nation's ashes
would sit on the table when roast was served
and the guests would think it was pepper

40 bullets & butterflies

we rub nations like catholic priests
rub the children of their flock

too many silly individuals
wear overall-striped
unconsciousness
rockin' blue balls
and silver chains around their wrist
as if slavery was ever stylish
those fools are childish
and of a lesser god
studying the TV as if the media was an evangelist

ludicrous lovers of wealth
measured in plated gold
rather than on the scale of one's soul
sold out
like old white Wonder
and rotten cheese
growing in the shady regions of our nation's asscrack

we act as if complacency has legs
and passiveness has toes
the bridge to middle America's comfort
is on Pinocchio's nose
it grows like Antarctica snows
like dandruff falls

if I had balls
the White House could suck them
and lick them dry
because too much time has gone by
in this fast food change line
where the blind flip burgers
and the content wash dishes
they wash away their wishes
as if they were leftover ketchup on plates
and play catch-up
with their debts and expenses
that shit is messed up

will the real slave drivers

stand up
and cough up
reparations to the civilizations
that they stand up
on proper payment
and all of that equality rhetoric
save it
I look over it like shit on pavement

I pay rent in a country
where fireworks take priority
over "minorities" in need
because this land was harvested from superiority and greed
it proceeds to be the way
in which people choose to succeed

they need the easy road
entitled Cheating Street in order to feel secure
but the nations that continue to pooper-scoop
America's bullshit
still endure

money may rule this world
and everything that allows it too
but I am the jackass refusing to climb this hill
refusing to let a bill
make me feel ill
towards another man's existence
like my heartbeat
my rebellion will remain consistent

I have blacklisted greed and jealousy
enlisted love and prosperity
as long as they're holding guns with me
I will blast into eternity
I am turning the lies we live inside out
exposing major ring
around our not so rosy collars
hollering to the people
to stop fighting
each other over a dollar

the scholars in the White House
have been studying our behavior for years

42 bullets & butterflies

they treat us how a frat boy treats beers
and how Mike Tyson treats ears

Paul Hunt

regie cabico

Born in Baltimore and later moving south to Clinton, Maryland, Regie Cabico was raised by conservative Filipino parents. While his two younger sisters were named Faith and Charity, Regie means "King," leaving no Hope in the family (his parents didn't know they had a Queen instead).

During his high school years, he never paid much attention to poetry and thought Sylvia Plath was a fashion designer. However, he did appreciate good acting monologues and enjoyed the work of Tennessee Williams without being fully aware that it was poetry. Regie was active in the drama club and credits his acting teacher for giving him the opportunity to work in sophisticated plays such as *Wait Until Dark*, *Stalag 17*, and *The Mousetrap*. Regie entered and won dozens of speech and oratory contests, unaware that he was preparing himself for his future as a slam poet.

While attending the acting program at New York University's Tisch School of the Arts, he felt discouraged by the lack of roles offered to young actors of color. He was tired of playing Chino from *West Side Story* and decided to give up performing altogether when he picked up The Poetry Calendar at St. Mark's Bookstore and saw an ad for poetry workshops at The Writer's Voice at The West Side Y.

A production of *for colored girls who have considered suicide/when the rainbow is enuf* and the proliferation of poets and anthologies that were being published at the time, inspired Regie to write some of his first poems, which he submitted to the workshops.

Under Agha Shahid Ali's guidance, Regie quickly learned the elements of craft and had a binder full of poems. He read at every open mic he could find.

One of the places he discovered was the Nuyorican Poets Cafe. Back then, the Lower East Side neighborhood was not as trendy as it is now. When Regie Cabico first stepped into the Nuyorican Poets Cafe, with its huge brick interior and bar, he felt like he was in a saloon and tumbleweed would roll past him. That night, there was a poetry open slam, and poets were being scored. Thinking it was all a joke, he entered, lost, and walked away feeling he would never win a slam competition.

Regie Cabico not only became a Nuyorican Poets Cafe Grand Slam Champion, but he also went on to take top prizes in the '93, '94, and '97 National Poetry Slams, with a 1st Place Team Prize awarded to his Urbana Team (formerly Mouth Almighty). He has received two poetry fellowships and a performance art fellowship from The New York Foundation for the Arts.

The slam was an exciting moment for him to come out as an openly gay and Filipino man. It felt exhilarating to be judged for who he was and what he had to say by strangers, while creating something rhythmic, accessible, and profound. Regie Cabico approached poetry slams as if belting out Broadway showstoppers. He soon became known for what he has penned "cabaret poetry," mixing elements of pure stand-up comedy, poetics, and dead-on Tina Turner impersonations (complete with wig and fishnets).

The *Village Voice* has described his work as "theatrically polished mixed with naked emotionalism wrapped up in a smarmy diva."

His first poems were published in *Aloud: Voices from the Nuyorican Poets Cafe*, in which Miguel Algarin's introduction described Regie as "a dynamo of metaphors spun out of an extraordinarily sensitive blend of gay audacity and Filipino sensibility." His poetry has also appeared in over thirty anthologies including *Slam, The Outlaw Bible of American Poetry, Spoken Word Revolution, The World in Us*, and *Returning a Borrowed Tongue*. He co-edited *Poetry Nation: A North American Anthology of Fusion Poetry*.

Television credits include *Stateside*, PBS's *In the Life*, and *Russell Simmons presents Def Poetry* on HBO. He has also toured with Lollapalooza and was featured on the "Free Your Mind" Spoken Word Tour, where his performance earned him a thirty-second spot on MTV.

Theatrical credits include *RegieSpective, Faith, Hope & Regie, onomatopoeia and a quarter life crisis in 1 act* (which won a Top 10 Play Citation at the 1999 Seattle Fringe Festival), and *Rhythmicity*, a spoken word play developed for the 2003 Humana Theater Festival at The Actors Theater in Louisville. He is currently working on his latest solo play, *Straight Out*, directed by two-time Tony nominee, Reg E. Gaines.

As part of the first wave of slam poets to emerge in the early '90s, Regie Cabico is one of the pioneering forces of the spoken word movement.

the trick

3:47 a.m.
Last call for drinks
I stumble to his motorcycle
Ride the wind behind his back
My hair plays born to be wild

4 a.m.
Inside his apartment
is an enormous
tank of goldfish
Anthropology books
spill over a desk
(I'm glad there are no dogs)

4:21 a.m.
He unbuttons my shirt
licks my tit
slams me eagle
on the mattress

5:30 a.m.
I stare at his body
with my stain on his chest
"You're my best geisha boy"
he whispers, turning the halogen off

6:33 a.m.
The sky turns from purple to orange
as I walk home form the East to the West
to roll back on my bed

7:10 p.m.
he doesn't know that I compose poems
on a keyboard   that I wear eyeglasses
to work   that I spell my name
with one "g"   that I am allergic to cut grass

this is the vanishing act of the year

coming out duet

HI MOM HOW YOU DOIN'?	HI MOM HOW YOU DOING?
I'm fine	
	I feel like shit
I'VE MOVED TO BROOKLYN	I'VE MOVED TO BROOKLYN
The rent is cheaper	
	My boyfriend lives there
It's pretty safe. There are cops everywhere…	Body parts found in the trash compactor
I don't trash your letters…	I hate your letters. I rank them in
I read your letters	importance with my student loans
	& Publishers Sweepstakes
Including the Bible quotes	
Yes mom…I go to church	I haven't been to confession in 10 years
How's who? Matt my roommate	
from NYU…	I had an M. Butterfly crush on him
He's great	
	I no longer see him
Maria?	
	We broke up
Maria and I broke up	
	Maria's a fag hag
	a Barneys-shopping fruit fly
I'm sure they'll be other women	
for me	I'm a man in love with a man
I've actually started to write poetry	
	I'm a pansy poet
No it doesn't all rhyme	
	don't show her the poems
These are my poems	
A lot of these poems are very…	
avant-garde	gay homosexual airbrushed dicks
Transcendental	Walt Whitman Disney-loving
Revolutionary	masturbatory macho gender
Risky	bending Key West sunset orgasm
	stall sex ejaculatory lick my boots

regie cabico 47

butch boy

Vivid Very Vivid

friend of Dorothy–Richard Gere
gerbil anal intercoursing Truman
Capote out of the closeted...
Contemporary!

Contemporary

Contemporary

But they're good

Tell her. Give her the gospel truth.

Okay mom, we have to talk
When I was young
I went thru dad's porno mags
Buried under your wedding dress

I will never forget Suzanne
Somers' breasts

When I was an altar boy
I stole all the bread wafers

I gave Holy Communion to my
sisters

I took your copy of *The Joy of Sex*

Semen stains on the carpet

Don't mention semen
I mean SEE mom

QUIT YOUR GODDAM SINGING QUIT YOUR GODDAM SINGING

I'm a man in love with a man
I'm a gay man and I live with a man
I've always been in love with men

Brian Bradley from drama club
I wanted to take him to the prom

Ever since you gave me my first
Disney record player

Mr. Rink The Music Teacher

As soon as my poetry came out

I CAME OUT   I CAME OUT
It's one thing to be straight-acting
but when I'm writing
I can't lie...I write because I   called names I loathed & loved
loathed the conformity of
Catholic military school   Stuck between my teeth
                                  hiding from guys like me

Years cruising the streets in search
of men with long coats...hats

LIKE A CROSS

The only close contact was a
trail of cigarette smoke

You feel you lost your son
in an asylum of skyscrapers

PLEASE DON'T FEEL THAT
YOU FAILED A MATERNITY
TEST

But I don't want to have to come
home like I am the sick
Nephew Prodigal son
in designer clothes

Don't blame genetics, dad, god

My life has born a poetry no woman
could provide

If you listen to my words
You will never notice the absence
of bridesmaids being serenaded
by chords of rice or miss
the sound of baby footsteps
If you listen to my words fall
without the sound of stars
like grace of your denial
Don't ever think that I am not your son
or that I honor you any less

Here are my poems... love them

LIKE A CROSS
A Gethsemane I could not change

I swooned on cigarette smoke

I know how scared you are of this
world

PLEASE DON'T FEEL THAT
YOU FAILED A MATERNITY
TEST

Keep him away from the babies
especially
the boys he'll contaminate the boys
like sour milk

My poetry is a sacrament no
church would have granted

(SING DOXOLOGY)
Praise God To Whom
All Blessings Flow
Praise Him all creatures here below
Praise Him above ye Heavenly Host
Praise Father, Son & Holy Ghost

gameboy

He buys me a glass of bass draft and asks if i am japanese /
his remarks / you are the perfect combination of boy and man /

are you the hip, hot, hung 9 inches of fun / seeking the slim smooth
    smiling
authentically thai-tasting geisha guy on the side macho dancer looking
    for his lord
& master m. butterfly wedding banquet joy fuck club

i am not a korean dragon lady running down avenue "a" on heels
with a teapot between my legs shouting where's my tip gimme
    my trophy

you wanna play with me you can   just quit orientalizin' cuz i ain't
    gonna change
my cotton knit calvins for you or my mother if i lose i ain't gonna fry
    you an
emperor's meal

or throw you eurasia or butterfly you an opera   i'm thru giving sex
    tours
of unicef countries 3rd world is for hunger and fat sally struthers
i am not a teriyaki toy

a rice queen's dream   a bowl of soy sauce to dip yr meat in
i've long been the "it" in a rice queen phenomenon that's burned faster

than gin bottles thrown at the black of my skillet

games so old as jason & hercules / men fucking my body like fresh
    golden fleeces
they ride my boyhood on bikes in the woods and rape it & kill it with
    leashes spit
words in personal ads / those clever written puzzles

for fun they blood brother baptize my emotions
then martyr my sisters in the backroom basements

i'm thru with charades i'm thru with your malice & your riots
    like hopscotch

50 bullets & butterflies

i'm not gonna fight it / i am beyond being poker-faced / mysterious /
    submissive

wanted by you or a being who's glossy and g.q. queen gorgeous

you wanna play freeze tag? i'm frozen already / touch me you'll swear
i'm the ice man's ice monkey hit me / & watch the mah-jongg chips land
lust me i'll soon feel the back of your hand / play with me then
if you think the sweet that's left to the taste in my tongue is enough
& not bitter love me for this
i forfeit the game remove my makeup and call you the winner

letter to lea salonga

Dear Lea,

I heard you got your big break playing the title role in *Annie*. I, too, wanted to be Annie but that was too gay for the southern Maryland town I grew up in.

The music director of the church said that I could play the lead in *Oliver* but he died in a crabbing accident. I took up piano instead and always had dreams of being a big Broadway star like you.

When you did *Miss Saigon* I thought your voice dripped gorgeous notes that could only be defined as Filipino pop, expressive, clear & so pageant-like. Each note deserved a tiara of pulsating minerals.

When you did *Flower Drum Song* I noticed how you stared at the highest spotlight as if you were being abducted by aliens. You were stiff in every solo number. Your eyes glazed over so much it reminded me of Janet Leigh's showered carcass in *Psycho*.

You are too young to have ceramic eyes on stage. The only musical theater performer with that trait is Carol Channing and she's only alive because Steven Spielberg used her as a model for E.T. So loosen up and snap out of it.

With much admiration,

Regie

you bring out the writer in me

Your breasts are couplets
Your body is a sonnet
Your thoughts share my soliloquy
Your kiss is imagery
Your eyes are iambic
Your tongue is trochaic
Your touch is stream of consciousness
Your complexity is Eliot
Your neck is Steinbeck
Your stubble is cacophony
Your presence is from fantasy
Your brilliance is Ashbery
Your ass is assonance
Your penis   is epic
Your torso is a tanka
Our rambling is a renga
Your fucking is foreshadowing
Your sighs are the climax
Your orgasms are onomatopoeia
                onomatopoeia
                onomatopoeia
Your clinging is Sexton
Your ejaculation is sprung rhythm
Your testicles are testaments
Your backbones are stanzas
Your viewpoints omnipotent
I see you in epilogue
going
going
gone

letter to tia carrere

Dear Tia,

I am so sorry that your action adventure series *Relic Hunter*
got canceled. You were truly wonderful as an archaeologist detective
crawling through mazes and *Scooby Doo*–like castles.

Tia, Filipina beauty who displays so much candor on every talk show
you could sell candy bars for every church group in America.

You embody the hospitality that Filipinos are known for.
I'm sure you could even play a nurse on *E.R.* as well.

I almost had to go to the E.R. when I saw you nude in *Playboy*.

Why Tia! Was the cancellation of *Relic Hunter* so traumatic
that you decided to hide naked in a grass hut.

Your breasts were full as 32-ounce San Miguel beer bottles
but your skin was so brown it looked basted.

Lying on your side you look like dinner for 30 stranded boys
in *Lord of the Flies*. I wanted to place an apple in your mouth.

Why did you do it?! Posing in *Playboy* did not help Dana Plato.

If you wanted a career boost, do what Halle Berry did and have sex
onscreen with an older white guy instead of showing us your monster
boobs and shaved nipa hut.

Posing next to wooden bowls and bamboo sticks, you look
like you're having an orgasm in Pier 1.

I wish you so much more success though I know your star
like your legs is only spreading.

Love,

Regie

Steven Underwood Photography

shailja patel

Shailja Patel was born and raised in Nairobi, Kenya, a third-generation East African Indian.

In 1972, Idi Amin, military dictator of Uganda, Kenya's neighbor, forcibly expelled Uganda's entire Asian population. Following this, the Kenyan government introduced a wave of so-called Africanization Policies, which effectively barred Kenyan Asians from holding public office or public sector jobs, and placed severe limitations on their access to higher education and business ownership.

Shailja grew up passionately patriotic about Kenya, knowing all the while that she would never be considered a "real," that is, African, Kenyan.

Shailja has always been a poet and a storyteller. Words allowed her to capture what she saw around her, analyze and rip apart contradictions and hypocrisies of racism, patriarchy, global power disparities.

She remembers arguing furiously against injustice, in the classroom and playground, with teachers and peers, from childhood. She learned early the power of articulate rage, absorbing the knowledge that whoever controls language, controls terms of discourse, shapes events.

Shailja left Kenya to read economics and politics at the University of York in the United Kingdom. On an overwhelmingly white, middle-class campus, she rooted herself in the small feminist community and the even smaller lesbian and gay community. She co-founded a feminist newspaper on campus, wrote and spoke publicly for reproductive rights, and helped spearhead the local campaign to oppose the first Gulf War.

She discovered Pratibha Parmar, Barbara Smith, June Jordan, Suniti

Namjoshi, Adrienne Rich, Audre Lorde, and found in their work, permission for her own voice.

After college, the only way Shailja could get a work permit to stay in the United Kingdom was to join the London office of Arthur Andersen, then the world's largest accounting firm. She was terrified to return to Kenya, where homosexuality is still illegal, and Asians still a scapegoated minority. While in London, she found a South Asian queer community. For the first time, she didn't have to choose between being Indian and being queer.

Shailja began to read her poems in public at Hammersmith's River Cafe and the Centerpoint in Hackney. She also joined the Guardian Angels, reveled in combat training, and patrolled in London and Berlin. She took part in the historic first Gay Pride March to cross from East to West Berlin, after the Wall came down.

Twelve years earlier, her family had been sponsored for immigration to the United States by an aunt in Ohio. Shailja's new green card would give her the fundamental human rights she had never enjoyed before: the right of secure lifetime residence and the right to earn a decent living without immigration restrictions.

Shailja settled in San Francisco and began to write again. When the Bay Area slam teams swept the national trophy, she went to the victory showcase, and was blown away by her first taste of spoken word. She began to slam, and to win.

Notable wins included Second Sundays, the nation's largest spoken word event, and the Santa Cruz Slam Championship. She was the first South Asian to break onto the national slam scene, participating in two national slams, winning the Lambda Slam Championship, and featuring at the 2000 National Youth Slam Championship.

Her poems about Afghanistan, Palestine, and the impact of U.S. militarism aired on the National Radio Project and KPFA radio, generating responses from activists and academics worldwide. Her work has also been published in numerous anthologies, journals, and college textbooks.

Awards include an Outwrite 1999 Poetry Prize and a Voices of Our Nations Arts Foundation Poetry Scholarship. She was a semifinalist for the 2000 Emily Dickinson Award and the 2000 Nicholas Roerich Poetry Prize and a recipient of a Serpent Source Foundation for Women Artists Grant.

Shailja teaches and performs at colleges, high schools, prisons, conferences, and festivals across the country. Most recently, she has taken her work to a larger audience, nationally and internationally, receiving standing ovations at London's Poetry Cafe and Glasgow's Diverse Arts Showcase.

Shailja believes that words can inspire us with the courage to change the world. Enduringly grateful for the extraordinary privilege of a life as a queer political poet, she is sustained by the words of all who use their voices for peace and justice.

dreaming in gujurati

The children in my dreams
speak in Gujurati
turn their trusting faces to the sun
say to me
care for us nurture us
in my dreams I shudder and I run.

I am six
in a playground of white children
Darkie, sing us an Indian song!

Eight
in a roomful of elders
all mock my broken Gujurati
English girl!

Twelve, I tunnel into books
forge an armor of English words.

Eighteen, shaved head
combat boots —
shamed by *masis*
in white saris
neon judgments
singe my western head.

Mother tongue.
Matrubhasha
tongue of the mother
I murder in myself.

Through the years I watch Gujurati
swell the swaggering egos of men
mirror them over and over
at twice their natural size.

Through the years
I watch Gujurati dissolve
bones and teeth of women, break them
on anvils of duty and service, burn them
to skeletal ash.

Words that don't exist in Gujurati:

Self-expression.
Individual.
Lesbian.

English rises in my throat
rapier flashed at yuppie boys
who claim their people "civilized" mine.
Thunderbolt hurled
at cab drivers yelling
Dirty black bastard!
Force-field against teenage hoods
hissing
Fucking Paki bitch!
Their tongue — or mine?
Have I become the enemy?

Listen:

my father speaks Urdu
language of dancing peacocks
rosewater fountains
even its curses are beautiful.
He speaks Hindi
suave and melodic
earthy Punjabi
salty rich as saag paneer
coastal Kiswahili
laced with Arabic,
he speaks Gujurati
solid ancestral pride.

Five languages
five different worlds
yet English
shrinks
     him
         down
before white men
who think their flat cold spiky words
make the only reality.

Words that don't exist in English:

Najjar
Garba
Arati.

If we cannot name it
does it exist?
When we lose language
does culture die? What happens
to a tongue of milk-heavy
cows, earthen pots,
jingling anklets, temple bells,
when its children
grow up in Silicon Valley
to become
programmers?

Then there's American:

Kin'uh get some service?
Dontcha have ice?

Not:

May I have please?
Ben, mané madhath karso?
Tafadhali nipe rafiki
Donnez-moi, s'il vous plaît
Puedo tener.....

Hello, I said can I get some service?!
Like, where's the line for Americans
in this goddamn airport?

Words that atomized two hundred thousand Iraqis:

Didja see how we kicked some major ass in the Gulf?
Lit up Baghdad like the fourth a' July!
Whupped those sand-niggers into a parking lot!

The children in my dreams speak in Gujurati
bright as butter
succulent cherries
sounds I can paint on the air with my breath

dance through like a Sufi mystic
words I can weep and howl and devour
words I can kiss and taste and dream
this tongue
I take
back.

this is how it feels

when you go down on me
wind blows fragrant
through my garden
from your hungry lips
earthquake tilts my pelvis
chalice for your sips
your tongue a hot wet finger
separates my labia
as swimmer cleaves the water
as a seamstress slices silk
this is how it feels
when you go down

this is how it feels
when you awake
sleeping flushed-pink
clit child in her bed
you slide back
her fleshy hood
out she pops
all rosy plump
to sing
as you go down

your tongue now a silver fish
flashes up my narrow stream
your tongue now a matador
taunts rogue bull between my hips
and when your lips enfold my clit
grape so ripe she begs to split
her skin
a million vines flow burgundy
through every last capillary
my fingers rumba in your hair
living forest on my belly you
leave grape juice handprints
on my butt as I
birth your face
between my thighs

this is how it feels

when your tongue enters me
scarlet sacred blasphemy
sanctified profanity
three thousand years
of history
two inquisitions
fourteen million witch burnings
untold lobotomies clitoridectomies
Freudian armies
of male god prophets
stand at the gateway brandishing
weaponry howling
you may not
enter

you just grin
your wicked grin flick
a finger at
their din you slip
your tongue you slide
your tongue you plunge
your tongue up into me

it's true we really do
change the world
by fucking yes
the revolution
is our naked bodies
woman's mouth
on woman's cunt woman's lips
in woman's labia woman's tongue
in woman's yoni girl
sings orchards into vineyards
into joy laughs joy
into another girl's
garden

let it give
pat robertson
dr. laura
screaming slavering
wet dream nightmares

here between my legs

eighteen-wheeler trucks
turn cartwheels
skyscrapers fall to their knees
solar systems burn and shatter
pyramids give up their dead

eater of death

Based on the true case of Bibi Sardar, whose husband and seven children were killed at breakfast by U.S. air strikes on Kabul in October 2001. To date, it is estimated that over 5,000 Afghani civilians have been killed by U.S. military action.

<u>One</u>
They came as we ate breakfast, I remember the taste
of black market naan.
Zainab and Shahnaz turned eyes like whirlpools
as I sprinkled them
with precious water.
My children ate slowly,
tasting each crumb.
I remember the bitterness
in my throat.

Before we finished
the sky ripped open, vomited
death, everything
fell around us, everything
burned, a voice like a jackal's howled
Kamal Gohar Shahnaz
Sadiyah Zainab Zarafshan

It split
my head, I would have beaten it
into silence.

I raised my hands
to block my ears, my fingers fell
into the well
of a hole in my face,
the howling
came from me.

<u>Two</u>
Three days later,
in the shelter,
starvation and nausea
fought like mujahedin
in my gut.

Aziza, my neighbor,
shards of rubble
still in her matted hair,
showed me
a package. Yellow
like the bombs. With an
American flag.
She said:
They say it's food.

Her eyes twitched, her head jerked
her one remaining hand shook, spittle and words
jumped from her lips:
Food colored like
the bombs. For the children
still alive
to pick from minefields
with the hands
they still have
left.

And finally
I understood
the savagery
of a people
who would gloat
over those they kill.
I cried out
to the shelter roof:
Have they no mothers
no children
in America?

Three
On the ninth day,
after Aziza died
still clutching the pack
she refused to open, I
pried it from her
lacerated fingers, I

ate the food.

The blood and bones and fat

of my children,
in a yellow pack,
with an American flag.

Kamal — perfection, how you bruise
and scrape my abscessed tongue.
Gohar — diamond, precious stone,
now break my loosened teeth.
Shahnaz — princess, red gelatinous heart
of this monstrous American pastry,
I smear you on my mouth.
Sadiyah — blessed one, sink in my stomach,
stone of my womb, I take you back.
Zainab — granddaughter of the Prophet, peace
be unto him, and you, sugar
my saliva, prophesy
what comes to eaters of death.
Zarafshan —
Zar-af-shan, littlest one, I named you
for a mighty river. You taste now
of rancid mud, you taste now
of poisoned fish,
littlest one
you taste
of splintered glass.

Four
Their names will not be remembered,
they are not American.
Museums will not hold their relics, they are not
American. No other mother's
children will be slaughtered
in their memory, they are not
American.

But I?
I have eaten
from the bowels of hell,
chewed and swallowed
the fragments of my children
and now — do you see?
I am no longer human.

Now as every nation

seals its borders against us,
I will seal my body to pain,
seal my eyes, mouth, belly
to any hunger not
my own.

I rename myself
America. No love
no grief in the world but mine.
And I will keep them safe—
in the cracks of my teeth
in the pit of my pelvis
in the raw raw flesh
beneath my eyelids.

Kamal
Gohar
Shahnaz
Sadiyah
Zainab
Zarafshan

she said no

On March 9, 2001, Christopher K. McCarthy, 22, of Concord, New Hampshire,
a U.S. soldier stationed in South Korea, was sentenced to six years in jail for
beating to death a Korean bar waitress who refused to have sex with him.
(From an article in Asian Week)

I want to know how that feels
rampant power, blind entitlement,
all wrapped up in six
starred and striped
inches of bludgeoning penis.

Korean waitress equals
receptacle for GI sperm,
sewer for American relief,
what made her think
she could choose?

She said no
so I hit her
I hit her again
and she fell so I kicked her
I kicked her again
and I want to know how that feels:
rage rises
fist in groin,
torpedoes belly,
pythons intestines,
sprouts two wings
like god's own angels,
thunders bullets
through hands and feet.

I want to know what it takes
to beat a woman to death.

Did she count her savings that day?
Promise her son: *tomorrow*
if I catch enough tips, tomorrow
we'll buy your school clothes,
and yes, maybe this summer
we'll go see your grandparents

in the village...
Duh. I forgot
she's nameless,
faceless, voiceless.
Breasts, hips, vagina.
Slick black hair and
slick red mouth
and open legs and—hang on:
she *refused*
to have sex with him?
She
refused?

Did the earth stop turning?
Did the sun go out?
Did the stars and stripes
freeze on the flagpole,
shatter in the darkness?
She was a gook!
You know the plot—why
do I have to repeat it?

He has a name.
She has none.
He has a rank, a gun,
family, church, hometown,
high-school girlfriend,
He's the hero!
She's a walk-on.
So he had to kill her.
What else could he do?
She was changing the story.

I want to know how it feels,
when the story is you: roots
in your groin, flowers
up your belly, tendrils
your intestines, blossoms
two wings like
god's holy angels,
testifies righteous bullets
through hands and feet.

Bring in the scales:

Six years for McCarthy,
Thirty-one years of her life.
Wait! I'll put more on her scale:
the dream she had last night,
the ache in her feet from high heels,
strip of blue silk at her window,
history books by her bed,
incense she burns daily
for her grandmother, stitches
her mother had
after her birth—

the scale says: *Sorry.*
She was only a bar girl
who didn't know her lines.

I want to know how it feels, McCarthy,
when the story falls apart,
the slick red mouth
says no,
the faceless
grow eyes
that stare into yours.

Does it explode your groin,
slice a bayonet
up your belly,
strangle your intestines,
spawn two monstrous wings
like god's avenging angels,
shrapnel KILL
through hands and feet?

Because the story
must be restored, the story
cannot be changed, the story
is about
you.
And how did she imagine,
Asian bar girl, yellow void,
where did she get the idea
she could say *no*?

for death and other lovers

I.
you dreamed I cut my hair
you call me
in icy dark December London
from fifteen-below-zero Calgary
to say *please don't*

after you die
I will shave my head
down to raw stubble
tendrils of blood
translucent red
will spring
from every follicle
radioactive tentacles
will hiss
around my skull

II.
we talk of fucking death
that morning by the pool
of being fucked by death

now I lie
beside your cooling body
you and me
and death in bed
the ultimate
ménage à trois

So who's
on top? Who's
screwing whom?
Who gets to come
first?

III.
I punish my body
for being alive

punish my body
your virus writes itself
in my cells
my bones crack
invisibly
with yours

I run city pavements
crunch fragile joints
push blood through arteries
force muscle fibers
to painful cramp
scream at each limb
damn you
how dare you
live stay whole
healthy in me
when you rebel in her

IV.
the night your head
was a brown paper bag
of evil postulating agony
that angel dust might shatter
I prayed
give me her pain

next day
period cramps
first time in my life
clawed gnawed
sank vicious fangs
into my pelvis
under red silk power suit
I fought to not cry out
in the boardroom

You met me
at Embankment
happy blue
balloon of joy
from your pain-free day
I learned to be careful

what I prayed

V.
ways to deal with HIV
name remaining T-cells
Percival
Algernon
Cuthbert Twistleberry

cancer — make pets
out of tumors
Fluffy Fido
Rover — he jest
keeps on wand'rin'

joke about lung spots
liver blotches
can't take you anywhere, can I
you keep messing up
your nice clean organs

VI.
this is what I keep
of you

when I said
do you have to wear
that perfume
on your skin
it tastes so bitter

your eyes dilated
you said
do you know
how a dying person
smells

no
my darling
all I know
is death was the taste
of Estée Lauder's

Beautiful
on your neck

Shane Luitjens/Torquere Creative

shane luitjens

Shane Luitjens was born a Midwest son in central Illinois. His family moved often but never far, quickly compiling a history of divorce, second marriages, alcoholism, and cancer.

His interest in writing came early when paper proved to be the more stable relationship to have. Much of Shane's youth through college was spent overachieving by collecting national and regional accolades for both creative writing and journalism.

After graduation (and seventeen media internships), he abandoned a career in television news and discovered spoken word, which engaged a new element of the voice in his writing.

With spoken word, Shane gained national exposure by participating in the Slam circuit, but he gained most of his joy in developing project-based works on subjects like the sex industry in *Body Work, Singlehood, Bachelorette,* and self-medication in *Blood for Wings.*

During that time, he began to combine text and photography, in addition to starting his career as an award-winning graphic designer. These days, Shane works to actively learn new methods of production to further his interest in combining text and imagery.

Shane does not understand the world as it is. His work has always been immersed in the landscapes that languages give us to both connect and often misinterpret intention, success, failure. He uses language as elements of pattern (within poetry and essay) or as textures (within photography) to display dialogues we do not often have in our everyday lives. Shane thinks of them as exposing his own ecstatic intimacies.

His work has appeared in various places throughout the country, including *Revolutionary Voices*, *Suspect Thoughts: a journal of subversive writing*, and *Lodestar Quarterly*.

Today, Shane Luitjens lives in Boston/New York with his partner, working as a freelance graphic designer, photographer, and aspiring explorer.

hey straight boy (i'll fuck ya)

Wait right there. And I tie his feet to the floor—
and I tie his feet to split bedposts, a conjunction.
And. I promise to be as gentle as the conversation,
the back-n-forth stances we make while trashing
the host of these parties.

Out the window, there were worlds looking in
and out there with them, there were rationales
as enduring as the moment you kissed me
without kissing me, as if it were in subtitles
and we had to be told how we are feeling.

Watching your tongue on the lawless curve of my finger,
you won't tell anyone what a good time we had.

because i care

Don't take this the wrong way, but I think you should die.

I think you should die because it will help you become a better person.

I think you should die because dead people are famous like Emily Dickinson or Paula Friedrich. You may not know Paula Friedrich. That's 'cause she isn't dead yet. But she will be, and then you'll know her. All dead people are famous.

I think you should die because you would get to spend all day in the park.

I think you should die because your body, once devoted to science, might help prevent a terrible disease or give medical students a good laugh in urinology.

I think you should die because death is really a state of mind.

I think you should die because the Psychic Friends' Network says everyone you are still friends with says Hello.

I think you should die because it would give me something to write about. A sad poem with lots of heavy breaths and a sigh before screaming at the top of my lungs how angry I am that YOU ARE GONE!

I think you should die because it adds drama.

> Don't get me wrong. I value you. I empathize with your concerns. And yes. The world is a rough and terrible place with challenges that we all find difficult to overcome.

> I say: Why bother?

I think you should die because the government respects dead people enough to let them ignore traffic signals.

I think you should die because dead people don't have to listen to Britney Spears.

I think you should die because the world would get so much more done over your dead body.

I think you should die because it will improve our ratings this season.

I think you should die because dead people have nicer makeup and are always dressed up.

I think you should die because if heaven is such a wonderful fucking place that you can't wait to reach, you shouldn't waste your time down here.

> Be impatient. Be an overachiever. Be willing to take the plunge. Bite the bullet.

> Put both feet firmly into the grave and shut the door behind you.

I think you should die because you have so much to give this world after you're dead — and absolutely nothing to contribute right now.

the breakup poem, part 2:
swimming narcissus

I have thrown down the last straw,
Whispered the final bit of nothing,
Sweetly dismantled Cupid from nibbly limbs
And still find myself attached to you.
Opening the front of sentences with your name,
I challenge myself to put the mere mention
Of you at the end in front of periods,
The final assault against a frustrated comma,
The hopeful feeling that coming face-to-face
Would only mean correcting a lock of hair
And not complete infatuation, utter disappointment,
A prolonged circus sideshow with a pole-centered tent.

I must, in no uncertain terms, eat the water,
And admit the obvious: I will never love me
The way I loved me when loving me meant something real,
Something palatable, something I unsuccessfully hid
Under the table, in the closet, at every mirror.

Years of flirtations, those chance encounters,
When grocery bagger boys would smile at me with glasses
So brilliant—there were two of me. In elevators, eyeing my crotch
With the delicacy of a civil servant looking for a taxable offense.

It was insulting, rabid—
And I made self-love in the 7-Eleven bathroom,
I ran from the pumps, my name still embracing these lips.

Oh yes.
I still corner my phrases with your every move.

We made promises and lied.
Showed up late to my own meetings,
Picked up the tab too many times.
Left messages for myself
Asking how I've been
Did I get the flowers?
How is your father?
Do you still know the merengue?

You saucy tart. You boozy strumpet.
You brazen sex-swilling gutter tramp—
How my penis revolves around you,
How my penis involves only you,
How my penis became so excited

Is none of your business.
You know I don't care.
You know that I only say that because I am supposed to,
Because I want to believe I am sensitive
And endearing and over it. Over you.

You beautiful thing.
You beautiful in single hours.
You when you aren't wearing red or orange.
You beautiful mostly when I am not focused on you.
But when you are blurry.

And you understand, don't you?
You feel the same. You open your eyes and drink.
Like bringing dirty water to the mouth,
You fall in love
Again.
From storefront to storefront.
Each time perfecting a smile,
At the risk of drowning.

negative sex

Just so you know, I am not going to talk about sex.
There will be no masturbation jokes during this poem.
There will be no low-level pandering to the petty level of penis
        or vagina humor.
Please leave that woman alone because she does not want to have sex.
Not with you.
            Not with anyone. She will not even think about sex. Just
            another glass of beer and this poem.
We won't be talking about sex. I will not talk about sex and that
includes
            no further discussion about the things you can do
with your mouth, your tongue, your hands, and a small can of mint
jelly.
As a tax-paying citizen in this city,
I expect to be free from references to oral copulation and genital
        stimulation—
Spare me the occasional double entendre that might lead me
to conjure any images of finger-fucking or ass-rimming, sex with
        animals, sex at all.

I understand how you feel.
            So, I will do everything I can
                    and I can

            to stop your mind from these thoughts.
We'll talk about spring in the city, or a cabin in the woods,
            the crystal clear sheen of clean dishes or entertaining friends
with music and conversation
            or a placid lake, silvery light, Grandma on the porch with
lemonade—

Not fucking your sister while the family was away,
or the hand job in the vestry, blow job on the playground,
or the way Aunt Michelle nodded at uncle Ray when they caught you
with your first boner—
Nor will I clutter your head up with
            the millionth time your wrestling coach lingered a little too
long in the showers
            or the way your brother's girlfriend laid her hand on your
crotch when he wasn't looking
just to see you rise.

There will only be thoughts of the infrequent kiss or hug
and not the random act of bathroom sodomy

and I won't let you think that the person you are next to
has ever had sex, will ever have sex,
or should ever have sex,
'cause they shouldn't.
And I won't talk about it so that you don't think about it, sex,
fucking, banging, boinging, nookie.
Those are not words I am using to describe what you
should not

and will not be thinking
because thinking leads to nastiness
and in case you don't know what nastiness is,
let me tell you:

Sex is wrong. You should not have sex.
Stop thinking about sex.
I don't know how sex got into your mind in the first place.
There must be something wrong with you.

ugly as

She says she says she says
that we could never explore the body as if it were a beach in
    the Bahamas
with umbrellas flowering along her chest and a Boca Raton sandal
    hanging off her foot
like she hangs off my tongue — she says she likes my tongue hanging —

but sex would make sense with a boy like me if boys like me were sexy
and she runs into the other room to grab a picture that robs a mirror
of its place. I am faced to face the lips of a 14-year-old girl
with ample thighs masquerading as cheeks, fleshy folds,
a phone number book that, left empty, splinters into eyelashes

and from this, she tells me not to make her ugly. Ugly as
skinny girls in black dresses. Ugly as pockmarked cheeks
and saber-toothed grins, as scars and large bones. Ugly as
flat-chested prepubescence. Ugly as uncertainty, as bad karma.
Ugly as stringy hair or perms or nappy-headedness. Ugly
as skin that might have been blessed on the Rhine or in the Congo.
Ugly as languages with Rs like rolled hills, skinny desserts,
junks with high sails. Ugly as girls who have deep voices
and crunchy pitches. Ugly as fat noses and plastic surgery.
Ugly as government cheese, as a fortieth birthday,
as a girl in this picture says ugly is this.

She says she says she says
that we are unavailable emotionally and she slaps my ass
with the heel of her throat — you can hear her she says she says

This is why there are American girls and we are corners
searching rooms for light. But don't you dare say it.
Just shut up and tell me something beautiful. Tell me
I am August. Tell me that you like uncertainty. Tell me
there is nothing wrong with American girls —
There is nothing wrong with American girls
There is nothing wrong with American girls
There is nothing wrong with American girls

She says she says she says
that we could never explore affection this way,
her leg hanging in the air as if it were my tongue
the way she likes my tongue hanging.

a gentleman's guide
to the good gay scene

Start here:

drop your pants
drop your job
become a waiter/bartender/salesclerk
work two jobs
move to the South End, Dorchester, Capitol Hill or Chelsea
pay three times the rent for half the space
fuck your neighbors
get high
take poppers
fuck your neighbors' neighbors
vacation in Provincetown, Fire Island
buy a condo, a time-share
rent the hot tub
get drunk
visit the parks
(conveniently your pants are still down)
pick up something
and someone
visit the doctor
fuck your doctor
get fucked by the male nurse
go to a bar
try e
x
dream of making porn
ask the guy next to you in bed what his name is
forget it immediately.

Start over.

Angela Jimenez

alix olson

Alix Olson is a nationally touring folk poet and progressive queer artist-activist whose quick wit, fearless poetry, and charismatic presence sells out venues across the country.

A member of the National Slam Championship Team in 1998, she has been a triple-award nominee for the OutMusic Awards and is a recipient of a Visionary Award from the DC Rape Crisis Center for her exceptional commitment to the promotion of social justice.

She has also received a New York Foundation for the Arts fellowship and a Barbara Deming Memorial Fund grant.

Alix has appeared on HBO's *Russell Simmons presents Def Poetry*, PBS's *In the Life*, and WXPN's *World Cafe with David Dye*. Through her own label, Subtle Sister Productions, she has released two spoken word CDs, *Independence Meal* and *Built Like That*.

She has graced the cover of *Ms.* magazine and her work has been featured in *Girlfriends*, the *Advocate*, the *Lesbian Review of Books*, and the *Lambda Book Report*.

Alix Olson is driven by the hope that a true democracy depends upon the contribution of all of our voices, and is hell-bent on sharing hers.

Unafraid to tackle tough socio-political subject matter, she has given voice to unspoken sentiments, raising awareness of queer rights and the mistreatment of women.

One part peace vigil, one part protest rally, and one part joyful raucous concert, Alix ignites audiences everywhere she performs.

daughter

I'll teach my daughter to bang on anything that makes a beat.
She'll shake-a-boom, she'll quake a room
she'll paint her cheeks warrior-style, then smile
beguile you, turn you inside out 'til your guts plead guilty.

She'll be built like a truck, built to work you down
as she works herself up.
She'll make holes in the street in her ten-inch spike heels,
in combat boots, stilts, on roller wheels,
she'll stroll through Male Pride
Amazon Babes at her side.

She'll relinquish White Privilege
observe, be wise, she'll compromise
when the fire is stoked by other womyn's desires
but she'll never leave the flame.

All the same, she'll crave what makes her burn.
She'll learn her Cunt's good name—
the thick liquid lips, the small hot tip.
No more of this cryptic shit.
This Vagina will be known.

She'll park in all the wrong places,
make faces at police cars,
wind up behind bars, bust out big before serving her time,
fingernails full of this grime we call

Reality.
She'll dig her way through.

She'll pick her nose when she has to,
she'll scratch her ass,
she'll be a crass medusa child
a wild healthy fiend
she'll live in all fonts and all sizes
curly *q*'s, caps, italics, and bold.

She'll fold airplanes out of shredded *Cosmo*s and *Mademoiselle*s,
then pilot them to Never-Say-Never Land
where Peter Pan's gay and Wendy's

okay with it.

She'll wear thick braids, she'll shave her head,
she'll eat thick breads, she'll let her breasts flop,
she'll mop the floor like Cinderella, then with
Rebellion—Prowess—
she'll unionize daughters for a higher allowance.
She'll be male and female and
in-between.
She'll preen, then crack her mirror, crack a beer
and watch *Love Connection*.
She'll go for days without taking a shower
just to feel unchained ivory-slave power.

She'll want more than what she's "entitled to"
she'll watch through Nike commercials and she'll
            Just Un-Do It
ask who's making that shit, who's breaking their backs
keeping her breaking that
glass ceiling.

She'll do all of this.

And she'll do none of this.

And it's funny how we hide behind these daughters,
hide ahead of our own Herstories
scared of ourselves
scared of the world
scared of someone who made us
one way
or another.

Well, this time around, I'll be bound to my own
mind womb
in my own birthing room,
I'll squeeze out, squeeze out
each crimson thick belief
then eat each pungent, sweet placenta
and relieved,

I will tear up this country's
"Welcome to the World" certificate,
tear off my father's

father's father's father's
name,
I'll legitimate my own entrance into a
Thinking Existence.
I will birth myself towards
Resistance.

But no frantic tick-tock of this Biological Clock.
On my own time, Foremothers at my sides,
Sisters as midwives,
I'll cut my cord, head for that War.
I will mother myself into my own grown daughter
and I will call myself
a homegrown
woman.

cute for a girl

I told her she was cute.
She said, "You're cute. For a girl.
Look, I like you a lot, but I like to give head."
I lay down on my bed. I said, "Try me."
She said, "No, it's dick I'm after, darlin'," and She
Headed for the door.
I said, "If it's dick you're after darlin', try my
Top dresser drawer.
But I've got small hands," I said,
"They never go limp when I fuck.
I got girl parts myself, so I know where's good to suck."
She paused. I moved closer.
She said, "I'm not sure I buy it." But her nipples perked;
Her pelvis jerked. She said,
"I guess I'll try it."
She stopped, dropped, rolled, paused, turned.
And that night I learned
That skin is where this revolution gonna begin,
Touching one woman at a time, showing there's no crime
In feeling this good.
God would be a dyke if She could find someone to hold her,
Instead of holding her up as the dark image.
In the church of my bedroom
She stopped, dropped, rolled, paused, turned, spread,
Said, "Oh god."
"Yeah, darlin'," I said. "Anybody, anybody,
Any Body
Can bring you closer to Jesus."

america's on sale

ATTENTION SHOPPERS!!!
attention 9-to-5 folk, cellphone masses,
the up-and-coming classes,
attention sports-utility,
plastic-surgery suburbanites,
viagra-popping, gucci-shopping urbanites
attention george clooney–loonies,
promise-keeper sheep,
stockbroker sleepwalkers,
big investment talkers,
ricki lake–watchers,
attention walmart congregation,
"shop 'til you drop" generation,
ATTENTION NATION!
AMERICA'S ON SALE!

we've unstocked the welfare pantry
to restock the wall street gentry
it's economically elementary
because values don't pay
yes, american dreams are on permanent layaway!
(*there was limited availability anyway*)
the statue of liberty is being dismantled,
$10 a piece to sit on your mantle or hang on your wall
by the small somalian child
you bought from sally struthers
sisters and brothers, it's now or never,
these deals won't last forever—
AMERICA'S ON SALE!
(*restrictions may apply if you're black, gay, or female*)

and shoppers!
global perspective is 99% off
'cause most of the world don't count to us.
our ethic inventory is low
because moral business has been slow,

the values-company is moving to mexico—
and *ALL ETHICS MUST GO!*

it's a remote control america that's on sale

because standing up for justice can't compare
to clicking through it from a la-z-chair—
answer: jerry, montel, oprah
question: folks who really care!
      for $1,000,000,000!
in this new mcveggie burger world order
where the mainstream scene has an alternative theme.
sugar daddy and ginger spice
and all cultures spliced and diced,
that's what music is made of when
AMERICA'S ON SALE!

national health care is 100% off!
and medicare is in the 50% bin,
so you can buy—
      half an operation
when **AMERICA'S ON SALE!**
there's a close-out bid to determine which religion will win
all the neon flashing signs of sin.
the christian coalition is bidding high
shoppers, you ask WHY?!
who needs a higher power when you've got the purchasing power
to corner and market
one human mold.
that's right—real family values are being UNDERSOLD!!

and it's open hunting season for the nra!
there's a special uzi discount—only today!
gun control?! we say—
      fuck it! blow it all away!
welfare mothers are on the auction block again,
we're closing out this country the way we began!
so step up for our fastest selling commodity
no waiting lines for hiv,
condoms and needle-exchange are a hard-to-sell thing
      (to the right wing)
while **AMERICA'S ON SALE!**

we're selling fast to the at&t ceo,
he's stealing all utilities, he doesn't pass go,
and collects all the money anyway!
he's the monopoly winner 'cause he bought the whole board
and we bought the whole game
now no price is the same!

because inflation is up on the ceo ego
and power is deflated as far as we go:

nike bought the revolution,
and law schools bought the constitution!
tommy hilfiger bought the red, white, and blue,
          (a flag shirt for 50 dollars,
          the one being burned is you!)
marlboro bought what it means to be a man,
lexus equals power — so get it while you can.
maybelline bought beauty,
new york's buying rudy giuliani,
mastercard gold bought the national soul
broadway bought talent and called it *cats*
the republicans bought out the democrats —
they liquidated all asses in a fat white donkey sale —
now it's buy one schmuck, get one schmuck free
in the capitalist party!

and there's nothing left to get in the way
of a full blue-light blowout
of the U.S. of A!
there's a:
          no-nothing back guarantee,
          a zero-year warranty,
when you buy this land of the fritos, ruffles, lay's.
this home of the braves, the chiefs, the reds, the slaves!
so call **1-800-i-don't-care-about-shit**
or click on *www.FUCK ALL OF IT!*
to receive your credit for the fate of our nation —
(call now! interest is at an all-time low)

but hurry shoppers!
because america's being downsized, citizens,
and you're all fired.

dorothea tanning

There's this Dorothea Tanning painting
and the arm of the artist is barely breaking through.
There's a gash in the canvas, and that's how I feel standing here
    in front of you.
It's a furious grief
it's fear scoping out the mad
it's this submarine of artists launching towards their shore of sad.
See, we were all eaglespread under america's weight that day,
eyes starry, striped in steel bars, hate-studded
with the slogans and logos of manifest destiny,
shoulders slumped in homage to our shriveling, shuddering century.

As retaliation became our password,
and the username: three thousand lives spent
and the message sent was in jingoistic text
and we all got sick fast from the warnacular virus attached.
As F-16s quickly colonized our city
and brown deli owners scrambled for flag mercy
and activists gambled with emotional heresy
and the budget of the death toll was quickly tabulated
and balanced against capital and CIA fabrications.

See, that day grabbed us all by the collar of our questions
and held us hostage there
and to second-guess the quarter truths was a sudden double dare.
And still, we hacked up history like hair balls,
quiet cats on tiptoe
reaching towards subversion
flip-flopping on our tiny block
generationally uncoached in our courageous contortions
and sometimes it seems, there is nothing left to protect,
liberty decivilized, freedom kept in Dow Jones check.
As Donny and George grab the rings and steer us clear towards
    nuclear brink
and I guess I thought life was meant to be lived
but then again, I ain't been asked to think.

Since that day my sister crept from her publishing house
across the bridge and towards the highway
and my best friend balanced on a Brooklyn roof
as the silvering slipped towards a charcoal skyway

and my station wagon, for once, hushed her rush,
surrendered fire trucks to the freeway.
And this hot head leaned on her cool hood,
and calculated harm's way.
And her radio was mumbling and her cellphone was buzzing
and some guy somewhere was screaming something
and all she could think was "my god, are they okay?"
But she was one mile of water away
from where she could do anything.

See, there's this Dorothea Tanning painting
and the arm of the artist is barely breaking past
and the media screams "she is cruel, duped, and crass."
But I squinted, saw her fist, it was not clenched up to swing.
It's a gesture towards dissenting hearts, it is beckoning us in.
There's this Dorothea Tanning painting
and the arm of the artist is barely breaking through.
There's a gash in the canvas,
and that's how I feel
standing here in front of you.

warriors

The paper called me a warrior.
A bad girl. A bad example.
The paper said I smile big,
but I curse too much.
And it's true. I do
feel like a warrior just for making it through the day, sometimes
I feel like a fighter. 'Cause I fight
to keep the fighting away and, sometimes,
walking down the street is a scientific experiment.
Your body laid out, splayed out, just for them
to tamper with it.
But you know, I think it's those with the scalpels
who are really the rats.
They want to dissect your ass 'cause your brain won't hold still for
    them
under that slide marked:
"split and fill with bullshit."
Y'know, my ass don't fit under that glass
and my brain moves way too fast for that.
'Cause if this is a movement we're making,
we have got to get moving
in this crazy maze we've been handed, we've got to quit losing
    ourselves.
We gotta use our big fat mouths to talk,
we gotta use our big thick thighs to walk.
We got to follow those who choose
a different way to knock,
those who banged with persistence
like the Audre Lordes, the Barbara Lees,
the Leslie Feinbergs, the June Jordans of my existence,
who chose a different way to walk,
took a chance, didn't prance, tiptoe,
twirl though this world.
You see, I refuse to slide past
even if it means coming in last.
I'm gonna stomp and rage and kick,
talk hard, think thick.
Y'know, it don't take a dick to have balls,
it don't take balls to knock down the walls
of this cheap joint.
You know, the point's hard to find with all these

ground-down passions.
But we've got a chance if we sharpen our visions
with our voices.
It's a choice to make noise, it's hard to be heard,
they'll toss you a muzzle wherever you go.
But baby, it's the waves that let you know
the ocean's alive.
So, we've gotta go deep.
Down past where your daddy found your key,
unlocked your knees
and took control
past where your brother cruised your borders
like some kind of night guard patrol,
past where the babysitter stuck a pencil up inside you.
So many ways they get you to hide you
from the world, girl.
We gotta go deep
we gotta use our black and blues like a second skin,
let our bruises thicken,
then begin again.
We gotta get up when we're pushed to the ground,
they ain't gonna hear us if we're screaming face down.
We gotta rise to double the size of our sound.
You know warriors are better
the second time around.

Kristal Mosley

maurice jamal

Originally from Oakland, California, Maurice Jamal is a Brooklyn-based performance artist, poet, writer, actor, and director.

As an artist he has striven to create new opportunities for the voice of people of color and the LGBTQ community. As such, he created "Sondays," California's first black spoken word series featuring gay men of color, and "Deepsoulpoets," the first male and female, gay and straight poets collective.

Fusing urban sensibilities with sexiness and rhythm, Maurice delivers his spoken word as a modern-day soul poet. His style has been described as being like "hot molasses...thick, raw, and bittersweet."

Through poetry events, theatrical plays, internet cafes, and appearances across the United States, he has built a reputation for "ear-catching" poems which capture the heart, soul, and beat of what it means to be young, urban, and black in the 21st century.

His spoken word CD, *Love Evolution*, was met with great critical success and was followed by his EP, *Your Ass Is Like Watermelon*. His latest effort is *Poetry Is Dead*, an exploration of sex, money, politics, and greed.

His first book is soon to be published by Tim'm T. West, author of *Red Dirt Revival*.

A Shakespearean-trained actor, Maurice has performed on stages from New York to Atlanta to San Francisco. Included in these works are performances with the national African-American Shakespeare Company and New York's famed La MaMa Experimental Theater.

Most recently, he can be seen on television on *Chappelle's Show* and the WB comedy series *Make My Day*.

Maurice directed the landmark play, *Up Jumped Springtime*, the only theatrical adaptation of the writings of Essex Hemphill. The play also earned the distinction of being the first all-black play for San Francisco's legendary Theatre Rhinoceros.

He recently filmed and co-starred in his directorial debut, *The Ski Trip*, a romantic comedy about the lives of urban gay men featured on MTV's LOGO.

A long-standing advocate for youth issues and disadvantaged communities of color, Maurice has also created programs for the National Task Force on AIDS Prevention, AIDS Project Bay Area, and Kaiser Permanente, among others. He is currently an advisory board member for the National Sickle Cell Health Network.

i write this poem

i write this poem
for the lonely boy
in oakland
sitting in math class
fantasizing about the older boy
the upperclassman
the senior
who sits in front of him
daydreams about lying on his bed
doing homework
the both of them
going over fractions, algebraic equations
adding and subtracting, adding and subtracting
while his mouth is on the older boy's body
finally seeing what all the girls
were whispering about

i write this poem
for the girl from ohio
who dresses like a boy
plays sports
with boys' toys
doesn't want to be a boy
yet imagines the joy
the boy
must feel
who's lucky enough to kiss
sarah

i write this poem
for 15-year-olds
who've found the courage
to simply be

i write this poem
for matthew shepard and sakia gunn

i write this poem
for carmen and kristal
shante and monica
brandy and ebony

girls who weren't born
that way
who met their end of days
at brutal hands
who were ashamed to admit that they
liked the way these girls kissed them

i write this poem
for the brooklyn and bronx kids
raised on the piers
on the waterfront
nyc docks
late night

i write this poem
for the kids
the children
hanging out in front of cabel's
and two potatoes
and traxx
you laughed at them
called them names
said that they were
too young to get in
but i saw you late that night
and i guess they weren't
too young to get into

i write this poem
for those who found family on the ballroom floor
strutting and dancing
striking and prancing
hieroglyphic ninja stances

i write this poem
for all the boys
who sling the slang
who use the word "bitch"
with surgical precision
who weave it
like some magical tapestry
into the voice of life...

saying hello at the beginning of the night

"hey bitch"
talkin' about the missed piece at the end of the night
"that bitch"
or just telling me that they loved my shoes
"Oooo Bitch."

i write this poem
for my house music divas
who move their feet
dance floor warriors
wielding conga drums and tribal beats

and i write this poem
for the dancers, painters,
singers, poets,
photographers, musicians,
the storytellers
whose art
incites
inspires
excites

i write this poem
for the gay boys and lesbian chicks
whose love life
has more drama than a loretta lynn song

for the girls
who like the taste of coochie on their tongues
for the boys
who like the taste of dick on their lips

i write this poem
for the acrimonious acronyms
that struggle to define life and living
the msm, glbtq, coc, npo, cbo, hiv,
std, gmad, bmx, cdc
support group
roundtable discussion
open forum
conference call
community task force
12-steppin' folks
on the front lines

i write this poem
for all those who engage in mating rituals
the throbbing
the pulsing
the pull
the lick
the pinch
the tug
the going inside
the sweet friction...
the release

i write this poem
for the lonely boy
in oakland
who sat in math class
fantasizing about the older boy
who one day
still fantasizing
still lonely
let's a stranger
who doesn't know his middle name
fuck him
and he feels love
as he is infected

i write this poem
for all the sissies and dykes
fags and butch femmes
lipsticks and queens
the closeted and the fierce

for all of punkdom
for all of lesbiana
for all of faggotry

i write this poem for me

the chase

i have been
        looking
                seeking
                        searching
                                for the right person
for a long time

i want someone sensitive
        someone caring
                someone mature
someone not afraid to be afraid
and let me see his fears

i've gotten tired of the chase

        you know…the chase

i see him in the club
and make eye contact
then i chase him around the room
to let him know i'm interested
i chase down the digits
wait at home for the call
and when we talk
i chase after him as he
runs around the subjects
of sex, dating, and commitment
when we go out
        he's late, or stands me up
i chase him down
to see
        what's up
                we finally hook up
                        then hook up
and i chase him around the room
trying to get him to put a condom on
at first it's all good
then after a couple of months
                        the sex is…
well let's just say
I've gotta

chase him down just to get a lil'
and when the relationship
is over
i gotta chase the nigga down
                    just to get my
                              shit back

                                        i'm really tired of reading

                                    i meet this amazing woman
                              but she won't return my calls
                i know she likes me
                        but she's playing all these games
                              sista tells me she's been
                                    reading *The Rules*
                                              she then proceeds
                                                    to read me
                                              because she says

                *"you need to learn to treat me
                like a strong, african queen
                and overcome the
                sexist, misogynistic, hateful attitude
                you learned from your
                father, frat brothers, basketball buddies,
                and all those niggas at the barbershop."*

                                              so i take her out
                                    to this fly lil' restaurant
                i read about
                        but she reads me
                              because she read
                                    the same review in *Essence*
                                              and says
                "you're tired for not having any originality."

                                    i'm really attracted to this sista
                                    and i know she wants me
                                              so we're

                        kissing
                        touching
                        rubbing
                        holding
                              and when the clothes start flyin'

                                        she say's
                              "stop!"
                                    sista tells me
                                        she's
                          "saved and sanctified"
                                    and begins to
                            read from the bible

                    why are
                    women
                      men
                      men
                    women

              afraid of an open, honest man?
                afraid of a strong sista?
                afraid of a gay relationship?
            afraid of embracing their lesbianism?

one day
i see
          her
              him

                    him

                          her

                    damn!
                    fine and
              just like i like them

                    thick!

              big breasted
              thick thighed
            racetrack runnin'
              ass on the back
                with that
              black man booty

              thick lipped
          dominoes and spades
              playin' spade
              dozen readin'
              kinky hair

bowlegged
just thick

thick
salty
sweet juice
sticking
to my chest

relationship? booty call?
dating? sex?
emotional? physical?
mind fuck? just fuck fuck?
relationship? booty call?

booty call!!!

lips
licking, kissing, wetting
hands
holding, touching, caressing
arms
holding me down
legs
between them
raising up
sliding inside
wrap me up
dick me down
let me in
let me out

breathing becomes panting
panting becomes sweating
sweating is salty
then
sweet
sticky
then
cold

lying
next to a stranger

on top of my sheets

things would be easier
if i was

gay
straight
lesbian
happy

i have been
looking
seeking
searching
for the right person

for a long time

i want someone sensitive
someone caring
someone mature
someone not afraid to be afraid

and let me see his fears

i've gotten tired of the chase

you know...the chase

almost

if i cover my ears
i can almost hear you
with your new lover

giggles and sweet nothings
about nothing
in his ears

i can almost
hear his voice

a voice that
doesn't sound like mine
doesn't need to hear
i love you
just every
once and awhile

doesn't need to ask you
all the wrong questions
like i used to do

where were you last night?
who was that calling at 2:30 in the morning?
why do you smell like china musk
when i wear cinnamon and myrrh?

if i close my eyes
i can almost see you
with your new lover

who does the things
i wouldn't do

his blackberry lips
shaped like mine
kissing your ass

honey-dusted brown
fingers
holding hands
and smiling thru

the bad times

if shut my mouth
i can almost taste
the things you're telling
your new lover

old lies
like fine wine
slipping down
comfortable
resting in my mouth

baby, you know i always work late on thursdays.
baby, you know that friday is my night with the guys.
baby, baby, stop trippin'...i was with my momma all day on saturday.
now, what...a brotha can't go to church on sunday?

if i hold myself
tightly
i can almost feel you
loving
your new lover

his body
soft and curved
still warm
from your touch
two days old

finding comfort
in an empty bed
covered by empty words
holding onto empty promises

if i try hard

hard enough

i can almost
forget
what it was like
to be me
with you...

almost

maurice jamal 111

oh, bitch, no

i walked outta the club
eyes wide shut
see, i hadn't seen my nigga
since i came in with my nigga
about an hour ago
now the club was over
but my baby told me he had ta
go to the bathroom
and he probably just got lost
on that long walk back
from the bathroom
in a club
we'd been to
a hundred times

now it was
last dance
last chance
last call
i called out your name
"baby...baby...where are you, baby?"

i was all
hyped-up and happy
stuck on stoopid
'cause i was stuck on you
"baby...baby...where are you, baby?"

your friends
joined me in the search party
looking
for my lost love
and then i noticed
a car in the middle of the parking lot
funny
it looked a lot like "his" car
but it couldn't be
'cause "he" was outta town
and even if "he" wasn't
"he" wouldn't be here
'cause everybody knew

"we" were gonna be here

so i approached the car
its windows getting steamed
as i was getting heated
so i knocked on the glass
and heard
you knocking
heard you
not talking
not speaking
but making sounds
on the groove
on the lowdown

rewind, so...
in the parking lot
outside of Cabel's
on a packed Friday night
you gonna ditch me
in the club
to fuck a nigga
in his car
as the club lets out
as a hundred niggas
are looking at me
to see what the fuck
i'm gonna do
your friends on the side
giving me that
"girl, i told you so" look
and then
like the snivly ass
coward you are
you take off
with this nigga
in his car
leaving me stranded
at the club

oh, bitch, no

sitting across
from you and your best friend

at the dinner table
i smiled wide
i felt warmth and love inside
because you
had finally had
that talk
like the proud, strong
man you are
you had picked up the phone
and dropped that other man
like the proud, strong
man you are
you had let him know
that things had changed
things had progressed
that all was good with
you and me
so when
that other nigga
showed up
at the restaurant
pulled up the empty chair next to you
sat down
and kissed you on your cheek
and you proceeded
to explain
how it was possible to love
two niggas at the same time
and that...
"the texture and complexities of our situations are different
and together, the two of you are like the two halves of my soul."
and that you hoped we could
all get along

oh, bitch, no

i remembered tasting you
my black coconut
round and hairy
my lips
working rhythmic
african
jungle acrobatics
till i

cracked the coconut meat
and tasted that
coconut milk
runnin' across my lips

i remembered eating you
my mango seed
parting flesh
like peeling fruit
and finding tropical
ecstasy
in the searching
and the reaching
and the stretching
of my tongue
inside you

so when i found out
that your sister
that you're living with
who shares your last name
is an intricate part of your life
'cause that sister
is your wife!

oh, bitch, no

we had met
about 3 months ago
and he was fine

about 5 foot 6
with a tight ass
and pretty dick

caramel-colored brotha
cornrows goin' back
body was like "ta-dow!"
i mean, nigga had an 8-pack

truth be told
it wasn't love
it was lust
it was about the cum,

the nut, the bust

but it was lust of the very best kind
we shared each other's bodies
but we also explored each other's minds

we talked about religion and philosophy
and the state of hip-hop

man...we used to do the cutest thing
we'd have picnics in my living room
set out a blanket
good food, good wine
our sweaty bodies lit by candlelight
we started to grind

so my phone rings one day
and there was a woman on the other side
she asks me if i know rasheed
and said "yeah, bitch, why?"

well you coulda bought me for a penny
'cause girl, i was done
she told me the boy was 16
and asked me
"why you fuckin' my son?"

oh, bitch, no

oh, bitch, NO
oh, BITCH, NO
OH, BITCH, NO

whether
butch or banjee
fag or hag
lesbian or has-been
top or bottom
we have all had an

OH, BITCH, NO moment

brought to you by
the tired and the faithless

116 bullets & butterflies

and the cheating and the lying
and the scared and the confused
and the wounded and the damaged
men
women
boys
girls
lesbian
homosexual
bisexual
trisexual
faggots
dykes and
trykes

who have not found
the ability or the words
or the language or the
inner peace that is necessary
to engage in loving
respectful relationships

in other words
the niggas that lie

we have all
been there

sometimes you are angry
oh, bitch, no

or confused
oh, bitch, no

or sad
sitting alone
surrounded by old photographs
oh, bitch, no

and other times
you are simply outdone
and like the true
diva-queen-lesbian-butch-fag
that lives in all of us

you simply clutch your pearls
pitch back your head
and give it to the children
like Alexis Carrington-Colby-Colby-Dexter from *Dynasty*

OH, BITCH, NO!

D.L. Weber

cheryl boyce-taylor

Cheryl Boyce-Taylor was born on the Caribbean island of Trinidad, in the town of Arima—a small scenic town nestled between mountains, hills, and a huge silver clock tower that everyone called "The Dial." It is in that place that she first felt the pull of poetry, through the African-griot rhythms of steel pan and calypso. The political, social, and sexual musings of calypso freed her from the rigid, racist teachings of the colonialists that pervaded the Caribbean islands. To this day, her poems remain infused with dialect, the vernacular of her people.

At thirteen, Cheryl left her beloved Trinidad and moved to the United States without her mother. It was the most difficult period of her life. She missed her mother so much, she could die. Her mom was hospitalized on the day before she left Trinidad. The next morning before going to the airport, her uncle Alvin took her to the hospital to say goodbye. Even now more than thirty years later, the memory of that day still makes her weep. It would be one year before her mother joined her in America. Cheryl turned to writing for comfort. She believes it saved her life.

Quickly realizing how invisible she was as a young black girl in America, Cheryl held on to her roots for dear life. Reclaiming all she had taken for granted: steel pan, calypso, her brother, brown stew chicken cooking on de coal pot, long family days at the river, bush baths in her grandmother's outdoor tub, bitter coffee on her fingers. She held it all inside to feel protected and loved, these memories became the soil that made her poems bloom.

In the late '80s, Cheryl met Audre Lorde, who invited her to study with her at Hunter College. Cheryl was in awe of Audre's performance style, her fierce, intellectual, and erotic poetry, her status within the lesbian poetry community and the world at large. Audre Lorde demanded from her students everything she demanded from herself; her standards were high, and she had little time for bullshit and poor excuses.

Cheryl was so nervous on that first day of class, she became physically ill (in addition she had forgotten her poems at home). It was a very challenging and difficult semester, but by the end of the school year she knew she wanted to be a poet for life. She wanted to be a poet more than she wanted to be a daughter, more than she wanted to be a mother, lover, or friend. Audre taught her to use words as weapons. Cheryl is still trying to make good on that promise.

Today, Cheryl Boyce-Taylor is a poet, visual and teaching artist. Author of two poetry collections, *Raw Air* and *Night When Moon Follows*, Cheryl was also the recipient of a Partners in Writing Grant and served as a Poet in Residence at the Caribbean Literary and Cultural Center in Brooklyn.

Her poetry has been widely anthologized in various publications, including *In Defense of Mumia, Bloom, Poetry Nation, Catch the Fire, Def Poetry Jam: Bum Rush the Page, Callaloo*, and upcoming in *The Paterson Literary Review*. She holds Masters Degrees both in Education and Social Work.

Laura Boss from *Lips Magazine* says, "Cheryl Boyce-Taylor is an acrobat of poetry — leaping in dazzling, daring moves from poignant family poems to highly charged sensual poems. With amazing skill she balances poems resonant with clarity, images fresh and often startling."

the pepsi poem

For Cee

I.

When that girl said
I could give you up
faster than I can my Pepsi

I should have answered
with my knife
sliced the diseased tumor
grown disloyal along her stupid mouth

her throat buzzed
a wicked hornet's nest
my poet's brain coma heavy
locked in naïve-blue lovesickness

II.

our first storm of spring
exquisite bugle beads of rain
decorate your windshield

there's a silver mist in trees
when night sleeps
outside sky a dusty rose pleading

I miss you, she says

now even these hands have eyes
search her nape of neck
for spiderwebs
miss you, she says

all that can be broken
Is

convincing the body

Study the poem you wrote
when you feel like going crazy
lay naked on the earth
cover your shame with praise poems

cover the bright bay windows
curved around a cruel day
make curtains of your poetry

cruise the sky
cruise the sky
find that slight patch of sun

stack poems, two three five
at a time on top each other
add your tears
make a bewitching violet poultice
cover those wounds, child

gather acacia leaves
a dash of sea salt
two unruly beams of light

two drops of blood
from one left hand wedding finger
a fountain pen
three diamond nibs
seven wads of paper

keep by your bedside
one flask kerouac
nine sprigs lorde
three june jordan candles
two tablets clifton

ten wads neruda
three large jars perdomo juice
five reams bonair-agard

one skillet two teacups
two steel pans

mountainous garlands of
ai ai ai

your reflection
study your reflection
use as mirror rainwater
keep calabash full

trace your mouth
lips deformed and bleeding
praise that mouth and swear
swear to love yourself

study your reflection
watch your eyes
look for crossing buffalo
clear a path ten quick breaths

your heart
strike your heart
strike it, child
let it break break
strike it
beat spontaneous poems
from wrist hips
lips fingertips

heart
beat violent
irreverent basin blue poems
beat poems from legs
chest eyes breast

now read read
damn! like a poet

crazy:
cheryl's rant

things that drive me crazy
bush liars wars
nanny-driven baby carriages
politicians   maria groper and arnold swastika
celebrities who use media to make their careers
then sue for *privacy*

starbucks
when they hide the equal
starbucks with their burnt overpriced coffee
myself for buying starbucks coffee

things that drive me crazy
the transit system
the sound system in the transit system
fare hikes
folks who beg on trains
folks who cuss their kids out on trains
men who spread their legs wide...wide as whores

crazy
crazy white girls on crowded trains who cross their long legs
all in your space and shit
folks who let their backpacks
bump you in the face and never
ever notice you are there

crazy
faggy boys who think they are cuter than girls
crazy black folks with blue eyes
white folks with nasty-ass dreds

spanish boys who flick their long hair more than white girls
more than diana ross   more than britney
more than the whole goddamn rodent-eating osbourne family

things that drive me crazy
lovers who treat you like shit
then dog you out for dating outside the race

nail salons   filthy street vendors   crazy
business owners who neither speak or understand english
caribbean bourgeoisies   food stamps   baby daddies

things that drive me crazy   poets
rags and tatters poets
queer eye for the weird style, honey
get over it...it's oh so sixties

who drives me crazy   poets
poets who read the same fucking poems for 5 years
and keep getting on slam teams
getting on slam teams   slam teams   slam

poems that reek of integrity
and their owners have none
poems that end with bitch and shit
poems that end with peligro

fish, who thinks because im'ma mother
i should retire my pussy
guess da nigga ain't never heard
about female sexual prime

and crazy poets who say
oh cheryl...you're like a mother to me
when my own child thinks of me as a friend and artist...
and, like no...the biggest titties don't always feed all the world
sometimes the titties need feeding *eh eh*

and i'm so over the pretentious poets
who are not really poets
who run around saying
gosh golly gee! you know how we poets are
late all the time
you ain't late yu trifling

things that drive me crazy
poets that rhyme sky with i
and blue with you
and fuck with cock   *gag!*
and me with me me me
dude, take a class   some are free

and it really, really makes me crazy
when somebody everybody anybody
say, i'm a poet
no...you're not
you read aloud   trash!

and i really get crazy
'cause now it's so chic for employers to say
wow! we have a poet on staff
yeah, what are you paying them
have they medical coverage
can they feed themselves
and their dogs

yes, their dogs
crazy crazy dogs
whose owners let them do their business on the sidewalk
or let them run crazy without a leash
or let their crazy dogs run up on you

then i say, are you fucking crazy
and they say
look lady, don't get crazy
my pookie is harmless

why are you acting so crazy
you hate animals or something
and i say no, you're crazy for thinking it's okay to let your dog run loose

and it really really drives me crazy
when he pulls his dog away
and gives me that poor-crazy-old-black-lady look

and i want to scream
this is a crazy filthy city
with shit and stink

and dog owners who look like dogs
who kiss them in the mouth
who love their dogs
who love their dogs
more than they love humans

and i love this crazy city

and poets and trinis
and pan   insulin   boys
world music   rum bread pudding
rollover minutes fresh lilacs

lavender oils   american girls
hot tubs   foot rubs and
my lover's rubber duckie
and rainy mornings stained with the sticky taste
of your sinful mouth

in the village underground

underground in the village
of this veiled city
where the subway does its iron dance

air removes itself
from bodies grown thick
and sweet with sweat
eyes round and hard
dull as rusted metal

underground there is a fear inside me
heavy as a hand
beneath our city
the music of river runs in stages

collides with nightmares
and all our dreams run together
the dull hooves of silence closing in

it is raining in my village underground
family woes run together
slick as sewer rats
not one goddamn thing
matches this wail

one begs money for homeless
offers food
she looks hungrier than most
one begs money to break dance
body contorts into seizures

newly out of hospital
another begs money for
medications

with bells and maracas
four men beat drums
sing poetry evoke Yoruba

their women drill white
wail in spanglish

call Ogun, Ogun father of metal
road master of the underground

and all her saints
all her gods fall to the floor
i know her eyes
i know that call

there is a fear inside me
heavy as a hand
my second skin
a flaming city

auction

i sat mute
in the marketplace
skin fading becoming one
with the dirty black walls

everybody talked at once
shouted screamed pitched prices
measured my square angular head
stained-white milk teeth

measured bustline, nipples
weight height shoe size
i sat blank, seized

all around swirling over my head
the gifts of christ
cross bible cock whip white man chains
laughter of the slave gods
my terrible sin unpaid

ankle weights neck chains
unhooked removed
washed, scrubbed down
as a wild horse

key turns in massive silver lock
sneaking glances
i marvel
my shiny specked obsidian smile

for my comrades

For Billy Fogarty

something's rumbling tonight
loud noises a car firing off
a tire   an uzi   a 9-millimeter

and i want to take the crazy ass
#4 train outta here
bus   plane amtrak   any
thing

something's jumping off
someone's jacking off
let me say there will be no more
riots   no more move bombings
no more fucking bussing
no more mumia   no more biko

i will not sit at the back of the bus
will not keep my mouth shut
rage is essential
i carry it like the babies
i can no longer bare

you want my nappy head
and all i want
is the music of wind

listen to my drum
i am trinidad's daughter
first offspring of shango

pass me a cup of ganja tea
and excuse me goddamn it
i am tamarind woman
tempering earthquakes under my feet

i cut my hair in full moon
root it under banana bush
pin bullets to my petticoats
wear grenades in my shoes

rage is an aphrodisiac
i ride your fear
like an oversized cock
be afraid

this is a warning
i will not be silent
i will not sit at the back of the bus

there will be no more grenada
no more panama
no more tupac shakur

something is rumbling tonight
there will be no more apartheid
this is not the old south africa
i will not keep my mouth shut
i will not sit at the back of the bus

come whisper, my comrades
rip my ache like sad storms
until they lay down my body
until they lay down my pen
whichever falls first

plenty time pass fast, fas dey so

1.
i used to kno when mango ripe
an ready to pick
i used to wait for guava
to turn from a hard green ball
when it yellow and cream ripe wid sun
i'd drag a chair from de gallery
stand up on it an full meh mouth
wid de sweet meat right from de tree
now dat was livin

ah used to kno
if meh grandmudder left hip hurtin
rain comin
an if she right hand damp
it go be sun in de mornin
rain after lunch

dem days chiren would sit out in the hot sun
for hours   me din kno notin bout tannin lotion
in we house when it come time for goin out
if yu skin did real dark an pretty like mine
man dey shinin it up wid coconut oil
so everybody for miles could see you comin

an dem nasty old men
dey seein yu first
dey crocodile eyes on yu lil breast
yu eh even kno yu hav yet
an if yu lil chubby huh
de grin gettin more wider
de calypsonian say
is like de bigger de better
de more de merrier
ting was nice tho

2.
dem days pas fast fast so
we leave an com new york
well   if yu see me up here

in dese people country
ah hav four lock on me door
ah runnin three job
an still cahn see whey de money goin

queens geh hard hard
ah pick up me fas self
an move to chelsea
chelsea was a place for sunday brunch
all you can eat and drink for $13.95
gay   modern   post post modern and retro

"you don't have $2,500 finders fee?
sorry, honey — this water closet will be gone
by midday" and it was

chelsea was a place for hard white cocks
stirring pain my black pussy could never fathom
hard boots open shirt pierced nipple
and a lil doggy collar fastened to de cock ring
i got tired of walking behind flat ass
weighted down with money
de damn gucci backpack bumping
carelessly in meh face

who fader know this one fader
who kno dat one fader
who runnin de exxon corporation
dat one is a lesbian avenger
who will proudly use daddy's
platinum card to make bail

i'm tired of this fucking, privileged,
politicallycorrectfakedfuckingfreedom
harlem is still a tourist attraction—

3.
if yu see me in dis place
time pas fas fas fas so
i eh ha time to study rain
never mind sun
meh left hip hurtin
but it eh predicting notin

i want to hold my friend letta's hand
at water's edge
transcribe the news waves tell
i want to braid olga's hair into a tree
fuse her roots backbackback into black soil

i want to play dominoes with donna and linda
make soup for keith when he's sick
draw a bush bath till billy's fever breaksbreaks
I want my family back

i want to sit and rock you
have my hips predict you coming
sit and rock you back to a time
when we sought respite in each other's breath
i want my family back

and i am blown away
in the loose dust that is this city
this house of confusion
these rooms of deceit
we have come to know intimately

i want my family back
in your absence   i am havana
speaking spanish to port au prince
i am papiamento speaking wolof to curaçao
the shrill spaces your withdrawn hands
leave in my body carries dull knives
and cracking trees

at this bewitching hour
i hold out my hands to you
somehow these empty nights
seem the right size for making homes

my tongue is heavy with its own lacks
i hold out my life to you
'cause dese days   dese days
duz pass fast   fast so fast
so fas so fasfas so —

cheryl boyce-taylor 135

Leo Toro

emanuel xavier

With a name whose translation is "God is with us, God is light," Emanuel Xavier was born in Brooklyn to an Ecuadorian factory-working mother and a Puerto Rican father he never met.

At sixteen, he was forced to leave home after an abusive boyfriend outed him. The West Side Highway piers and Manhattan's gay discotheque scene became Emanuel's home, and the legendary Houses of New York City replaced the parents who had abandoned him. During this time, Emanuel relied on hustling at the piers as his means of survival.

A chance meeting with a gay cousin, who gave him housing, was the catalyst that set the stage for change. Emanuel completed high school with honors and addressed his graduating class as president of student government. He went on to pursue an Associates Degree in Liberal Arts at St. John's University.

However, these accomplishments soon gave way to engulfing bitterness of the past, which included sexual abuse as a child. He started using drugs and became a dealer at some of New York's largest dance clubs. Interestingly, at the same time, Emanuel began writing, perhaps to understand the insanity of his life and save himself from self-destruction.

Inspired by his newfound ambition, Emanuel saved up enough money from his drug profits and traveled to South America for several months where his first book was born.

Emanuel's return to New York marked a new beginning and a transition toward the literary stage. Avoiding the entire club circuit, his new life's emphasis became poetry. He began reading at various open mic events throughout the city and met many key performers and promoters of the spoken word poetry circuit. Regie Cabico became his first mentor and teacher within this new arena.

Emanuel first published two of his poems as postcards, returning to the same clubs and streets he once sold drugs and tricked at to personally hand-distribute them.

His first poetry slam was at the Nuyorican Poets Cafe at the urging of his date, poet Carlo Baldi. Emanuel won the audience over with a fresh and poignant brand of poetry that celebrated sexuality, Latino heritage, and the often-brutal streets of New York.

Pier Queen, self-published in 1997, was Emanuel's debut collection, which included many of the vibrant and emotionally raw poems that earned him the Nuyorican Poets Cafe Grand Slam Championship.

In 1998, he founded the House of Xavier, a collective of poets and writers that would fuse ballroom culture with spoken word and host the annual Glam Slam.

By 1999, his semiautobiographical novel, *Christlike*, was released and became a Lambda Literary Award finalist.

Years after he first graced the stages of smoky cafes and independent theaters that made up New York's underground poetry scene, Suspect Thoughts Press published his second collection of poetry, *Americano*.

Emanuel Xavier's poetry and prose have also appeared in *Urban Latino Magazine, James White Review, Long Shot, Men on Men 7, Besame Mucho, Virgins, Guerrillas & Locas, The Love That Dare Not Speak Its Name,* and *Bad Boys*.

He is also featured on the spoken word CD, *5 Past 13 – a little bit LOUDER: Volume 1*.

Emanuel has appeared on the award-winning *Russell Simmons presents Def Poetry* on HBO, hosted PBS's Emmy-nominated newsmagazine, *In the Life,* and co-starred in Maurice Jamal's feature film *The Ski Trip*.

He has been awarded the Marsha A. Gomez Cultural Heritage Award for his contributions to gay and Latino culture and received a City Council Citation for his contributions to the City of New York.

Emanuel Xavier has openly revealed himself and his life through words and poetry with the hopes of inspiring others to express themselves without regret or fear of prejudice.

the hip hop in my heart

If
you were my lover
I'd worship you
like a lethal white trash Jesus
lick you from dirty boots to shaved head like a lollipop
inspire hip hop rhymes to drop on the mic
fancy myself a rapper's delight
dangling like a diamond and platinum chain around your neck
charm the pants and everything else right off you inside the limo
going down until you shoot in my mouth the way Lorca would rather
    have died
and glance a wicked smile dripping with cum
reflecting innocence not stolen by the streets in your eyes

I'd be your bitch
I'd be the cute little Latin boy standing next to you
outside the trailer park in a brown and white photograph
dress in all the banjee clothes stored away with the past
And while you fucked me
I'd speak Spanish and watch
you growl like a furious dog

How delicious we would be
like the taste of white-chocolate-covered peanut butter
picturesque like a snow-capped mountain
featured in magazines like Benetton ads

I'll kiss you on the lips next time
so that you'll think of me as more than a friend
Mmm, the sweetest smell is your breath
Mmm, the sweetest smell

If
you were my lover
I'd get your name tattooed across my back
listen quietly as you talk about yourself
without saying a word about me
which, you should know, is really difficult

I understand your need to travel
meeting other fans in Massachusetts

Chicago   California
Texas
Florida

In the meantime
I'll have enjoyed several sushi dinners with you
hustled my way into your heart
bottled your scent
studied your moves
So when you're away
I'll find you in these poems

the reason

Because you tried to kiss me on the first date
in the front row of a crowded theater
before the movie started,
after snorting cocaine in the bathroom;
because of those arrogant eyes,
glazed by self-destructive frustration;
because of those futile lips
forcing against my face
assuming a crucifix or winning lottery ticket;
because of that smirk, revealing egotistical conquest
like another prey, a kingdom to possess
as if the gods had sanctioned your spell:

The residue in your nostrils damaged your view
with misguided judgment,
my love is a tree existing alone on a mountain
less like a forest
and definitely not one for you to smoke.

in the eighties

My eyes in the eighties
never saw death nor sorrow
no parades of pride from those lonely at night
no broken heart like pieces of glass on the ground.

My eyes in the eighties
saw the crumbling piers where young colored boys were bought,
the dog's collar, the poisonous powder,
and indestructible towers illuminating empty beer cans
from the back seat of stolen cars.

My eyes reflected from the stare of anonymous men
on streets where cats hunted mice
on alleys of lust, with cold hands and groans
penetrating as their children slept.

Walls where sprayed paint immortalized names and legends
rivers that swallowed the secrets of intercourse
in the place where dreams were meant to die
my journey began there.

Don't know how it happened. I suppose
I was never meant to get this far.
There are places that nurture noble men
but my eyes, disguised behind shades —
no innocence to find.

outside

Hypocrisy exists in our world today
when those that are out can only go so far
and society is surprised when those who prefer to hide
react with violence to threats of opening closet doors
because, in darkness, they are safe from those responsible
for reducing our brothers and sisters to dust and memories
like Matthew and Brandon and Sakia and way too many others
      to name

Those of us that are out, in these empty rooms,
dance ignorantly to the occasional drumbeats of liberty
while the only difference between us and those huddled
in corners and shadows of fear
is that we have a little more space to breathe
yet the smell of equality is only truly found outside
where there are no limits or debates on how to legislate desire
and sexuality is simply the right to physical expression between
      consenting adults

We could live out of the closet but we could never leave this house
monsters, especially those with hideous diseases and colored skin,
are not welcome in the open fields of America
where others could dare to dream of marriage or adoption or
      political office
or defend our country from imaginary weapons of mass destruction
because not all of God's children are worthy to see the light
beyond these cold white walls
we are only tolerable as long as we remain silently lingering indoors

Straight friends sometimes visit to feed our hungry souls
with stories about journeys and adventures
taking the time to join us and mourn the memory of our dead
before heading back into the privilege of sunlight
leaving us behind to wave goodbye from gated windows
unable to come out and play
if only we could run past the prejudice and feel the wind across
      our chests
discover lands starving for diversity and star-filled skies awaiting
      to shine for us too

In the distance, the emptiness of towers fallen,

a cruel reminder of our perversions and sins
as preached by religious men with tongues that are holy enough
to lick the innocence of children
to touch the openings of children
while faint sounds, unrecognizable as cries, emerge from
      underneath closet doors

There are too many of us in this house
located on a land far away from Normal
chanting songs of freedom every day
We only want to be outside,
we only want to be outside,
we only want to be outside,
The Lord is outside

It's no wonder some would rather die moths in the closet
when butterflies are not free

clean

Lathering you
in the shower
after sex
Washing away
the trace
of our desire
the sins
of our world
Spilling
like secrets
Abuela's lagrimas
baptizing
this union
this purification
of soul
With these hands
a poem
I draft
across your chest
along your back
below your waist
before
you lift me up
lock lips
to drown
my tongue
with your sweet taste
the taste of me
the taste of us
together
healing
the wounds
sealing
the scars
Mi amor,
there is a war going on
outside
but beneath this rain
the only pain
is the knowledge
that there is a drought

Sooner or later
we must turn
these faucets off
return
to the reality
of people thirsting
for our blood
If only
we could stay
until the children stop dying
until mother's stop crying
until our skin wrinkles
like daddy's did
like daddy's did
Mi amor,
the water is warm
feels like being
inside your arms
Through the drops
in your eyes
I see a glimpse
of peace
a glimpse
of love
& I
am finally clean

a simple poem

I want you to continue writing
because I will not always be around

With lips that will never touch mine
read your poems out loud
so that the words are left engraved on the wall
make me feel your voice rush through me
like a breeze from Oyá

I want to hear about Puerto Rico
about sisters with names like La Bruja
about educating youth about AIDS
I want to hear about life in the Boogie Down Bronx
surviving on the Down-Low
don't leave out stories about men
you have loved and still love

I want you to write poems that you will never read
press hard on the paper so that the ink runs deep
hold the pen tight so that you control the details
prove to me that I inspire you
reveal yourself between the lines
hear my praise with each flicker of the candle
write a poem for me

Do not choose a fresh page from a brand-new journal
use paper that has been crumbled and tossed
thrown out by a spineless father only to be recycled
save a tree for future poets to write under

Rewrite me into someone more attractive
stronger than life has made me
make me tough and sexy, aggressive like a tiger
stain the pages with cum, lube, the arousal you find
at the sight of naked boys, draw me sketches
bring the words to life with images
make me a man with this poem

Read it in front of the audience
with hidden messages just for me
be real and tell me why

I am only worth a haiku

Your epics are meant for others
I already know,
use red ink to match the blood from these wounds
with brutal honesty
let me die with your last sentence

Then resurrect me with rhyme
read from your gut
let me hear the wisdom of *mi abuelo* in your voice
let me find my father in you
remind me of all the men that left me broken promises

In your eyes I want to see a poem
when you bring me to tears
with painful memories
buried beneath your thick skin

Between teeth gapped like divas,
I want to hear quotes from books
I never read

Make me believe you want to be a poet

Make my heart break,
tell me why you could never love me
with just a few words
leave me lost and insecure
feel the admiration of others
bask in their desire
forget that I am there

Pound your fists in the air with passion
go off about politics, poverty, machismo, and hate
scream poems that don't give a fuck
about traditions, slamming, or scores
save your whispers for those who make love to you

Write a poem for me that makes me want to puff a joint

A poem that loses control
unafraid to be vulnerable
for once just make me believe

it is all worth letting go
when the smoke clears
I will understand
the reason
I am just another face
in the crowd

I want you to continue writing
because I will not always be around

legendary

In memory of Pepper LaBeija

There are Gods amongst us in these ghettos
so black, so fierce,
so brown, so beautiful,
their time on earth may be as oppressive as ignorance
limited to the demons flowing in their blood
but after safely passing over back to the clouds
the wind will still carry their auras and prophecies
their bones will still beat drums for their children to dance to
the phoenix will still rise from the flames of Paris with hope in womb

There are Gods amongst us in these ghettos
so brown, so fierce,
so black, so beautiful,
that if you spend too much time caught up in yourself
you just might miss Him that is goddess, she that is god,
        they that are legends
working the runway as if walking on water
reaching the stage to that promised land
where "peace" is not ridiculed and the only war worth fighting for
is protecting your child from the terrorist acts of a mainstream
        America
where "reading" is an act of learning
not degrading words used to disguise fragility and fractured dreams
where "shade" is a shadow you walk in to avoid the light
but who wants to stay out of the warmth of the sun?
if you waste your time trying to be a false prophet
robed in attitude and labels to obscure the insecurity
you may fail to recognize their divinity and miracles
parting the crowds, resurrecting from the floor, scoring tens
        of commandments,
because trophies will not feed the hungry, coat the homeless,
        hide the scars,
Grand Prizes will not bring Lazarus or LaBeija back from the dead
they will just sit in your closet, fake idols gathering dust,
before the gold paint chips away
you cannot sell them for freedom
you cannot trade them in for love

There are Gods amongst us in these ghettos

so black, so fierce,
so black, so beautiful,
so brown, so fierce,
so brown, so beautiful,
watch them carefully and say your prayers as they enter the ballroom
angel wing feathers decorating skin recrafted over silicone
        and martyred colors
see the Gods dream, see the Gods give, see the Gods live,
they exist in the spaces where white is not the only hue that
        represents purity
they will not battle to your rhythms and beats
click, spin, and dip simply for amusement
they will not teach those who share their souls and names to hate
their heartbeats are louder than the blaring speakers

You want realness...look at your hands
are they red from the revolution or from the blood of your own sisters?

There are Gods amongst us in these ghettos
so black, so brown, so fierce, so beautiful, so bright
look up towards the heavens and pray
then look at yourself in the mirror and say
"Stars are not only found out in the sky but in ourselves"

Reverend Michel St. Germain

daphne gottlieb

Daphne Gottlieb was born in Philadelphia to parents who seemingly lived the American dream. Her father grew up poor in the Bronx and, through hard work, became a doctor; her mother emigrated with her family from Europe during the Second World War. She grew up in Upstate New York.

Although she excelled in school, being raised by urban, leftist, Jewish atheists in a rural, conservative Catholic and Christian community made her schooling an alienating, disturbing time for her, as she felt very much the product of exile. She found solace and pleasure in books and writing, and her first poem was published at the age of eight.

Around the age of thirteen, Daphne began auditioning for and performing in musical theater. The community surrounding the arts thrilled her, and she found herself immersed in a vital, thriving milieu.

A girl who she met (and who was the object of her first real same-sex crush) introduced her to punk rock, and Daphne was rapt: she began collecting albums and listening on her headphones to the college radio station deep into the night. She also became aware of herself as queer around that time, though she couldn't find appropriate descriptors for her experience for at least a decade to follow.

She also began reading and writing poetry feverishly, in earnest, and won a number of local contests with her work. One piece of her writing caught the attention of her English teacher, who sent her to speak to the guidance counselor out of "concern." Both she and her parents were outraged. She began hanging out in the nearby college town, graduated high school early, took classes at a nearby university, and snuck into nightclubs.

Daphne attended Bard College on scholarship, and majored in Creative Writing. While there, she was the co-editor of at least three student start-up publications, and was chair of the entertainment committee.

Between her junior and senior year, Daphne's father contracted lymphoma—the disease he wrote the first medical research study in America on—and died. Daphne finished college and wrote a creative thesis, in part entitled "Jokes and the Unconscious," about the institutionalization of medicine and her father's death.

After college, Daphne spent a year in graduate school for journalism at the S.I. Newhouse School of Communication, but left, after being consistently baited by faculty, and being told that her story ideas (which included such "wild" ideas as interviewing sex workers to provide a point of entry to discuss sex work and make a small, fragmental attempt to decommodify bodies in the workplace) were "bizarre." She moved to San Francisco with her then-boyfriend.

Although the relationship ended soon after, Daphne's love affair with San Francisco persevered. She worked for a national magazine for six years, during which time she became Senior/Managing Editor (at night, she volunteered and worked at an all-girl sex club, go-go danced at a queer bar, and generally misbehaved).

She also became injured with a repetitive strain disorder from her day job, and was partially saved from hopelessness and day job word-sickness by Red Dora's Bearded Lady Cafe, at which the legendary Kris Kovick was curating spoken word shows. Daphne suddenly remembered that spoken word/poetry was something that she *did* and stepped up to the mic.

She never stepped back. She was the first girl to read at the revered Sister Spit, and began featuring around the Bay Area. She left the editorial field thanks to the RSI and burnout, and finished writing her first book (which was published by Odd Girls Press in 1999) and became enmeshed in the local poetry slam scene.

She competed representing the San Francisco Mission District at the 1998 National Poetry Slam in Austin, Texas. Her first national tour followed, as well as a spate of regional tours. Rededicating herself to her writing, she pursued her master's degree at Mills College.

Her second book, *Why Things Burn,* was published by Soft Skull Press in 2001, which was celebrated with a second (inter)national tour. A third, *Final Girl,* which is centered around the last girl alive in horror movies, and which, in part, chronicles her mother's death from lung cancer, followed in 2003. The book, published to wide acclaim, inspired yet another tour.

Daphne lives in San Francisco. She is working on a number of top-secret projects.

for suicide girls who have considered extensions/ when manic panic is enuf

when a hand tangles her hair
that's not her hair at all,
she giggles, bats her night-ringed eyes
and pulls out bright blue ponyfall extensions
corset laces hiss and busks crack
false eyelashes strip
tender, butterflies kissing against pale cheeks

together, breathing deliberately,
fingers steal and smart
into the pile of discarded girl
heaped on the floor
this fresh frankenstein fuck:
fingers snag in twisted fishnets,
garters snap back at black fingernails
petticoats hush and aah and the eyelashes flutter and fly
until the corset bones burst
and everything
together
goes
limp and

it's so quiet
with two naked girls
snarled together
on a couch their arms full of their beloved
naked clothes,

one color of
smeared lipstick
in the dark.

liability

One late beautiful afternoon, as everything in my apartment glistens, gilded with early fall sunlight, the moon-eyed mewling of my cat tells me we're out of cat food. I am also out of people food. The gorgeousness of the day has inspired me, made me giddy, and so I decide to go to the store dressed as a girl.

I pull a long blonde wig out of a drawer and slide it over my head, shake my long, gold tresses at myself in the mirror, smile my pink frosted lips at me, flutter my eyelashes, thick as bat wings. I shimmy into a tube top and miniskirt and slap my favorite fuck-me pumps on my feet. It's not just a grocery store trip — it's a celebration.

As I walk the few blocks to the store, swinging my purse, everyone seems to be in a good mood. The girls at the bus stop in front of the fast food restaurant are slapping each other's hands, stopping to suck on sodas, yelling, *Miss Suzie had a steamboat, the steamboat had a bell...* Women smile at me as I pass by, and men tip their hats, say "Good afternoon." I decide I want a steak and a beer. I run the list over in my head. Steak. Beer. Cat food. I make it into a song, sing *steak beer cat food* while I walk.

The grocery store is large and clean. I admire the towers of glossy fruit, the towers of neon cereal boxes that rise into the air. I sing my list to myself as I toss stuff in my basket. *Steak. Beer. Cat food.*

As I leave the store, it's twilight. The buildings have grown taller from their day in the sun, and the shadows crawl along the streets, quickly growing longer. The sun is going down fast, too fast, and there's a breeze, cool and strong as water, blowing, that threatens to pull the wig right off my head, whips me in the face with acrylic strands.

Cars pass by, slowing, honking, yelling something that I can't quite make out and don't want to. I walk faster, try and push the wig out of my face so I can see where I'm going, one hand on top of it, one clutching my groceries against my tube top. As I pass the bus stop, something suddenly hits me in the middle of the back. I turn around. It's the girls who were playing hand jive, but they've all grown to be seven feet tall. "Sorry, it dropped," they jeer, pointing to the empty soda cup filled with ice from the fast food place. I turn around and walk faster. Another cup hits me square in the back of the head, knocks me off balance. The wig slides over my face, and I blindly teeter and stagger along.

I have a new song now: it's sung very fast and it goes *only one block from home, only one block from home* and I'm singing it into the puffy clouds my breath makes. *Only one block, only one block* when I hear a man yell YOU FUCKING FREAK YOU FUCKING PUNK and there's a smash against my eye suddenly I'm on the ground, rib cage smashing against the hard can of cat food, beer bottle shattering under me as I skid on my face. Instinct pulls my body into a tight question mark as I look up. There's a cocked fist in my face that belongs to a red-faced man, all teeth and rage. I whimper and suddenly his fist unclenches, and he takes a step back, freezes. There's blood running down my raw cheek. He and I stare at each other.

Slowly, so as not to startle him, I pull the steak from the shredded bag, rip open the plastic, and place it against my eye. The man is stuttering, aghast, slowly taking the tiniest steps toward me, stuttering, *I'm sorry, I'm so so sorry, I thought you were a guy.*

living legend

"Dream as if you'll live forever. Live as if you'll die tomorrow."
— James Dean

being james dean
isn't easy
even james dean
couldn't do it for long

so now it's mine
to be the kind of boy
girls want to fuck
boys want to be

boys want to fuck
girls want to be
to fuck
james dean

in the leather bar
bathroom, putting cigarettes out
on his arm
ashes to ashes, dust to

that kind of tough
come-on-and-prove-me-
right-here rough
come on

with fingers too fast
for "please," knees
smacked on the tile
nose full of piss

and clorox, handful
of your hair,
see, that's
the kind

of james dean i am,
i see the way you look at me
when your cock is in me
james dean

the way you cry out
when my knuckles find you
slick inside.
one step past tender

is where you find raw
and that's where
we're driving
tonight

where i find you
in me,
james dean
when we

fuck on the barstool james dean
against a chain-link fence
james dean, rebel without a
daddy's on his belly for you james dean

momma's on her back
and now i'm taking baby
for the ride
of her life

straight from my james dean hips
with curves as sharp
and dangerous
as a rebel boy's death

watch us as we go
as we are one
two
one

red hot tail light flares
side by side, rolling up to the edge
as we scramble
as we soar

as we rush, as we push, as we go
as we crash right over
as we james dean, one
into

one
faster
than the speed
of death

suicide artist

So I'm in love with a suicide artist. She's going to be famous someday. She might be here right now. I'd tell you her name, but you'll know it sooner or later, see it in the newspapers. I'm just hoping it's later, not sooner.

She's dedicated. She studies her craft night and day. *Dying is an art*, she says. *Guns aren't lawful, nooses give*, she says. *I am vertical*, she says, *but I would rather be horizontal*. The cabinets are full of bell jars. She piles rocks everywhere in case she feels like filling her pockets with them and running into the ocean. *That smacks of plagiarism*, I tell her. She snarls at me, but she knows I'm right.

Every day begins with orange juice and a pint of vodka, as she pores over biographies of Plath, Woolf, Hemingway, Sexton. *Is hemlock illegal?* she asks. *Is arsenic?* By noon she has a cigarette lit in both hands and gets confused trying to turn pages. By two, she's under the house with a handful of pills. By three, she sings quiet songs to herself without words, plays with piles of cigarette ashes on the kitchen table. *This could be me*, she says. *This could be you.*

By four, her head's in the oven. I do all the cooking these days. It's too dangerous to let her near the knives. When I split tomatoes apart like succulent hearts, she says, *Can you do that to yourself? Or does it always take someone else?*

I don't know, I tell her.

I could drive a car into a wall, she says. *I think it's been done*, I say.

You know, I tell her, *It's not too late to consider another career*, and she starts sobbing wildly, uncontrollably. She eagerly empties a bottle of tran-quilizers into her hand, eats them like candy, says, *If you believed in me, I could be great. I'm going to be famous*, she says. *I'm going to be the best…*

Shhhh, I say. When sleep fills her mouth, I walk back into the kitchen, cleaning up the cigarette butts, throwing the empty bottles, half-finished suicide notes into the trash. I eat dinner alone and crawl into bed beside her, put my cheek to her chest, listen to the breath she hates so much. Everything I love about her is what she hates.

That night, I dream of her, I always dream of her, lying beside her while she dreams only of her art. *Art is transformative,* she tells me, and my sleep transports her inside a car of her own invention, a sexy red racer with syringes for wheel spokes, an exhaust that spews cigarette smoke, a car that runs on pure vodka. She's revving the engine, she's popping the clutch, she's rolling straight down the hill, too fast, heading straight for me.

She's got no brakes. There's no time to move out of the way. I stretch my arms in front of me. I'm not sure they'll be strong enough to stop her. There's a smack of body against metal, blood on the windshield, the smash of head into glass. We're kissing. My mouth is full of blood, and I can't tell whether it's mine or hers.

calliope

I've got a thing going on with a magician's ex-assistant. Things ended badly between them. After the rabbit died, he pulled a disappearing act, leaving her sawed in half in the black box. She's trying so hard to pull it together, but really, she's a fraction of the woman she once was. Two halves, to be exact.

Which is not without its benefits: Sex with two people has never seemed more like a threesome; it's even worth the bloodstains on the sheets left by either half of her waist, but it's hard to watch her getting dressed afterwards, dragging her top half towards the bottom, sliding herself almost whole. Sometimes after sex, her top slips off walking to the bathroom. Her legs, not seeing, blindly stumble on, tripping heels over head on her way back to bed. She gets back in the sheets; arms, then back; ass, then heels; she aligns herself and meekly says, "TaDaaa."

People will tell you that love only breaks your heart, but it really can break you all over: in half, in quarters, eighths, sixteenths. I tell her she's lucky he didn't leave her after the box-of-swords trick—the one where she's in the black box, but he sticks sword after sword into diagonal after diagonal across her tender body—or the metal blades trick, where he divided her into quarters. *It could have been so much worse*, I tell her, *but you are such a strong* woman, and she nods through her sobs, staggers towards the bathroom for another tissue to wipe her eyes with. I'm not sure she knows it's true. I think all she knows is that it feels like hell right now, that it's hard to heal when you fall apart, bloodily, time after time, hour after hour, day after day. *Strength*, she says, *is its own kind of curse. It's so hard to keep myself* here, she says, balancing her upper body carefully on her lower. As she bends for a Kleenex in the dark, I am thinking of other girls, the girl I loved who fell in love with a lion, lost her head over it—we just necked a lot; of the girl who fell in love with the tightrope, got addicted to getting high wired and nothing else was enough; all the beautiful, damaged women who have come through my life, and I wonder what would have happened if I'd met them first, if I'd met them before they were so badly hurt. All this time I thought I've been kissing, but maybe I'm always doing mouth-to-mouth resuscitation, kissing dead girls in the hopes that the heart will start again. Where there's breath, I've heard, there's hope.

I hear a soft slip and thud in the bathroom, a small, damp dragging as she recomposes herself. I hear her, through sobs, choke out, "TaDaa," and see the swell of her curves, upper, then lower, as she slowly, carefully, balances on her feet and walks gently back toward the bed, toward me, doing the proudest, slowest strut through the darkened room. She's lit by the confetti of carnival lights coming though the window from somewhere very far away.

Peter Dressel

marty mcconnell

In 1997, a public relations consultant with notebooks full of poetry realized she was so bored that she'd honestly begun to care about sports and sought out Cincinnati's only open mic.

Three years later, she took up knitting because everything else in her life revolved around poetry.

Six years later, she was tapped by legendary producer Norman Lear to co-create an unprecedented spoken word show to travel the nation and stimulate political activity among young Americans.

How does such madness occur?

Marty McConnell grew up a theater and word freak in the suburbs of Chicago, majored in speech communication at Miami of Ohio, and worked in public relations for four years before abandoning that career to hit the road with the Morrigan, a group of three Chicago female performance poets she co-founded in 1998.

The Morrigan completed three national "Wandering Uterus" tours (summers 1999, 2000, and 2001), setting new standards for multivoice performance and obliterating old ideas of what "women poets" can address and accomplish.

In 1999, she moved to New York to pursue her MFA in creative writing/poetry at Sarah Lawrence College, and was adopted by the poetry family at 13 Bar/Lounge in Union Square.

As a member of the 2000, 2001, 2002, and 2003 NYC/Union Square team at the National Poetry Slam, she became part of the louderARTS Project and eventually co-curator of the Monday Night Poetry Series at Bar 13, which the Project runs along with a series in the Bronx, ongoing workshops, and collaborative performances in New York City.

After completing grad school, Marty started working with Urban Word NYC (then Youth Speaks NY), directing the program that provides writing workshops, open mics and slams for New York City teenagers, in addition to performing her work and facilitating workshops at colleges around the country.

Her poetry has been published in numerous anthologies, including *Will Work for Peace* and *In Our Own Words: Poetry of Generation X*, as well as in literary magazines, including *Prairie Schooner, Fourteen Hills, Lodestar Quarterly,* and *Blue Fifth Review*, as well as in her own chapbooks and CD, *mirror/balm/glitter/glass*.

Marty McConnell has appeared on HBO's *Russell Simmons presents Def Poetry*, as well as on the *NYCslams* and *5 Past 13: a little bit LOUDER* anthology CDs.

The call from Norman Lear convinced her to temporarily leave her home in Brooklyn, her teen poets, and her louderARTS community, to write *Declare Yourself*, a collaborative four-poet show designed to tour throughout 2004 and stir the nation to political involvement.

Marty believes that poets are bridges to what we can't see yet, but trust to exist, that poetry allows us to transcend our regular level of existence, and from that vantage point see all things as new.

She lives at the intersection of worlds, aiming through her work to challenge the categorization and segregation society too often requires regarding sexuality, art, gender, race, and beauty.

all the way down

she starts with the hand that took
the letter that said *I love you.*
regrets the fingers, nails clipped
to the nub. the palm, love line jagged,
intersected every millimeter, mad highway
crossed and re-crossed. all the way
to the wrist / bites down / swallows whole
with a full glass of water, thumb catching

on the stomach lid / *good* she thinks
and starts in on the eyes that blinked at the word
love that shut to words *crush*
to *tenuous* to *breach* / regrets the lashes lying
impossibly small anti-moons
on that pillow, regrets the shedding and chews

the lips. lips that said *rules* that said *bad
idea* turned coward to lust and said
yes. yes to the woman she knew
she'd wound and did and now handless
eyeless can't answer the guilty phone can't fix
the betraying / the blasphemous lips
bleed like licorice all the way down

for warmth

I wanted to kiss her right then. not
on the forehead, after wiping
her tears—but on the lips, through the smoke
and bar chatter

but then what she with her fractured heart, I
with the lover, un-jealous, open / could we
kiss, give sex for comfort, heal
and grieve / how would we leave each other then

maybe it would be easy, morning showers
and talk of poetry and families, daffodils
on a kitchen table

my first was 19. ivory reed, clean and chiseled / two months
after her year as a prostitute, my family crumbling
at its center we held each other up on unpredictable nights
hoping some salvation could spark between drunken lips

in the rush to mean something larger, details often slip:
the man walking into a mailbox at the sight of us
holding hands at 7 a.m., feet coated in sand
after sleeping on the beach the night
she whispered her favorite Adrienne Rich line:
two women sleeping together have more
than their sleep to defend

birds tired from flight, wings bent, feet turning inward, we
are the walking wounded

one says weeks later, *I've never needed to be held*
the way I did that night and I remember the tightrope
of knowing she was bone and not porcelain but fissured
in places nonetheless, letting her remove
her own clothes and then mine, letting the moment
own us both with refusal to memory

one steps into my sleeping bag, small goddess of foot stomp
and song / kitchen floor, laughter from the open
bedroom door / antennae trembling, hands
eager to conjure grace from my simple frame / old pain of exile

and fresh pain of three friends' death in one week plain
as her knees curl to my stomach and we agree to *not now,*
not like this

one, 26, a friend's ex-lover, forbidden, anticipated
like Christmas, battered by the friend's paranoia
and cocaine habit, often cried after coming, heavy breasts
pressed against my arm I left her
confessing I'd fall in love if I stayed, knowing I've never
healed anything, just held pieces in place
while the glue dried

when one says another woman assaulted her, don't ask
if she fought back or why she was there or what
she was on don't ask if she said *No* or how
many times / drive her to the clinic
for the first appointment. lend her your car
every week after that.
the night she decides she needs
to be held by you, comes to you,
you'll be amazed at how she doesn't cry
but sleeps with her cheek to your chest,
how touch can turn weapon
and back again

we the tested / we the standing the slit and rebuilt
spot each other through winces and nonritual scarification,
carry each other across borders of too much whiskey
or too many lies for one lifetime, betrayals
too buried for words, symbol
and circumstance
we lean into each other like robins
spreading feathers / for warmth.

harder than flesh

you know the flesh is easy. it's the rest
that's hard—the balance of identity / society
/ morals / desire

—the thrumming behind your knees
that lingers days after you leave him
at the airport, nightly phone calls
only sharpening the ache

—the edgy scent of a dark woman's
perfume, the recognition
you could take a new lover.

every mouth, every bloodletting, every
blistering failure and unearned success
gave you something you need here

so you will choose—now.
in the instant of decision.
with her rapidly walking away.
knowing that to be one is simpler
than to be two, that those
who desire both, all, even together,
live in the liminal spaces
outside the comfort of labels
and limits

knowing you are too many
for the minimization, too broad
for the boxes

—could call yourself gay
except the man perched in the lobby
of your heart has grown essential
to your breathing

—could call yourself straight
except the woman in the fourth row
has a collarbone that makes your lips quiver

so you will choose.

when the man in the pickup yells
DYKE and your arms circles tighter
the waist of the woman
not yet your lover

when the gorgeous butch at the bar says
so what are you?   and you know
what honesty will cost you
when the voices in your gut insist the words
you have raised instead of children
will never outlast your brief tenure
in the spotlight

when you know you could never be enough for all
you would die for
and keep fighting anyway

you will choose

knowing morning is not optional
but waking is bravery

knowing the man in the pickup has a cousin
gathering the courage to come out
and she will hear you speak
two Mondays from now
and her chin will rise a bit

knowing all you can do
to get through this day
without running into the woods
or rush hour traffic is choose

what connects your gut   to your spine   to your heart

refusing to sacrifice any facet of your sexuality
on the altar of any cause, wearing the proof
of your life in the price your loud pen will exact

knowing this life is an argument with darkness, a battle
to believe that morning holds something
worth waking for, something harder
than flesh

real trouble

it doesn't get any easier, only different—
the knife slides to the right
missing the spine by centimeters
or miles, it hardly matters anymore

was it ever so bad? real trouble sticks like aluminum
to foil, not foil to frozen chicken

you were never good. hand over
the tin halo. you were a bent mirror, dancing versions
of what they wanted to be or see never you
or at least not all

what's lost in the translation
stays lost. mutilated intentions,
magnetic seconds of unadulterated
want—god, the lips the water the god awful
throat fire thirst—

uncalled witnesses for the prosecution
scrapped for their turn on the stand

all gavel and hips all ogle
and blame

now the kiss, the lunch, the calls
unrequested absolution give me a
fucking break trade your wings
for ink and write for once
something true
and bloody

stand on that stage gut-strung and sinful
featherless   mortified   holy

homeland

you're not safe. nothing stands between you
and victim status but whatever
has kept you whole thus far. your father can't save you.
your lover, the police, the government, suburbia, fear —
and your god's in his heaven meditating on free will.
at age seven I learned about nuclear war. that night,
I sat my five-year-old sister down
to share facts with her that had been so long
withheld. I'm telling you this now.
there will always be men unafraid to die
and take you with them. men play football
with pneumonia, broken ribs, hairline fractures
to the spine that threaten to leave them paralyzed.
they volunteer for wars over oil and pride, take up guns
against enemies and innocents alike for a government
that ignores their votes at will.
women have sacrificed their bodies
for uncounted centuries. in childbirth, for love,
for country, for god, dressed as men to fight those same
tainted wars, dressed as whores to survive — she too
will make you a martyr to her end. question:
if a man can disable a flight staff with a pair
of blunt tweezers, does he need the tweezers?
yet scissors are confiscated, nail clippers pitched,
laptops rattled and opened while tubes of hair gel
filled with enough liquid C-4 to take down a fleet
of DC-9s pass unexamined. cops study the driver's licenses
of pedestrians while warplanes drop food boxes
onto ground littered with landmines this is not
a new world. when have you been entirely safe?
when have you — woman, person of color, queer,
small man, rich man — walked the streets entirely
untouchable? a man tracked my movements from 1990
until he was jailed in 1995. I lived in Des Plaines, Illinois,
where so much nothing ever happens
the teenagers go to Park Ridge for kicks.
yet it bred John Wayne Gacy, who ate boys' corpses
for breakfast. yet it spawned Steven Josefow,
who when finally arrested possessed hand-drawn blueprints
of the houses of thirty-seven girls in the four
surrounding suburbs and had only recently been fired

from his job as a substitute teacher. there are children
in Afghanistan, in Bosnia, in Cabrini Green Chicago
who've known less than three nights in their lives
without gunfire or bombs dropping without real
and imminent threat to their lives. this is not
a new world. look at your hands.
are they red like mine?

i let you call me beautiful

I let you call me beautiful

because I know you mean beautiful
naked-faced / unshowered / raspy

because you mean raw / pen-in-fist / screaming

because you mean lustful / razor-tongued

I let you call me beautiful because you've traced
the scoliosis snake
of my spine, kissed the stretch marks
under each breast, stroked the lines
around my eyes

because these are my grandmother's eyelids
my father's lips, my great-great grandfather's cheekbones

but I've fed this face sunburn
and city air, callused the eyes
and let the brows grow in

for the sake of the veins that river my wrists
for the sake of the prolapsed valve in my heart
for the sake of the scars marking my gallbladder absent
for the sake of the rasp and rattle of my functioning lungs
for the sake of the prearthritic ache of my elbows and ankles
for the sake of the lifeline sectioning my palm
for the sake of the photographic pads of my fingertips
for the sake of the vulnerable dip at the base of my throat
for the sake of the muscles surfacing on my abdomen
for the sake of these arms that carry babies and anthologies
for the sake of the leg hairs that sprout and are shaved
for the sake of the ass that refuses to shrink or be hidden
for the sake of the cunt that bleeds
and accepts, bleeds
and accepts
for the sake of the prominent ridge of my nose
for the sake of the strange convexity of my rib cage
for the sake of the single hair that insists on growing
from my right areola

for the sake of the dent where the mole was clipped from the back
of my neck
for the sake of these inner thighs brushing
for the sake of these eyelashes that sometimes turn inward
for the sake of these hips preparing to spread
into my grandmother's skirt
for the sake of the beauty of the freckle
on the first knuckle of my left little finger

call   me   beautiful

kidnap the word from perfume bottles
and magazine covers
the way I stole back this body
from the airbrushed delusions I knelt to
in dormitory bathrooms

swear beauty means sex
with the lights on, means caressing
imperfections because this beauty is human
and human is flaw.

standing naked before the full-length
I smooth lotion into new cellulite
and old scars, close my eyes to picture my knees
my navel, my forehead / an architect
reconstructing the house
she grew up in

I believe in this body

like I believe in the beauty of plaid, the blonde swirl
on the back of my six-month-old cousin's head, the untouched
drape of snow across my windowsill, the wedding ring
on my grandmother's widowed hand

the way beauty is the color of joy
after suffering, the quick intake of breath
before Yes, the way fury is beautiful and orgasm,
beautiful, the terror of headlights as you spin out
on the ice, searing solitude: beauty

call me beautiful. I'll burn both of us down
to bone.

Andre Mason

travis montez

Travis Montez was born and raised in the Southern city of Nashville, Tennessee where he spent his entire life until coming to New York City for college in 1996.

The South still defines him in a lot of ways. He comes from a large family that goes to Bible Study every Sunday and has the big dinner after church with all the aunts and cousins stopping by for some sweet potatoes and uncles telling you stories about their childhood days. And that is where most of his poetry comes from — religion, family, old contradicting the new, romantic drama — that is the South.

Firm roots in the South notwithstanding, Travis made a life-altering decision when he decided to attend New York University. While studying for his bachelor's degree in journalism and Africana Studies, he discovered spoken word poetry at an open mic held on campus.

He had always written poetry but had never really performed it before. When he saw the poets onstage bring their words completely to life, his mind was blown wide open, and he knew it's what he wanted to do.

Months later, winning his first slam at the Nuyorican Poets Cafe in the fall of 1998 would mark his official induction into performance poetry. In front of those usually enthusiastic and often-intimidating Nuyorican crowds is where he began to develop his unique brand of poetry.

Dedicated to voicing life lived at the cross sections of American race, gender, class, and sexuality, Travis has garnered a reputation as an artist willing to tackle the harshest moments of life and shed light on topics that society is often afraid to touch.

He goes where the hurt is. As a writer, he feels he lives where people are most uncomfortable or try to hide behind blinders of ignorance. With many of his poems, his goal is to force a conversation or prevent people from saying they didn't know of a certain reality.

This focus has led Travis to pen powerful poems about a father's murder of his gay son, the rape of a close friend, and his own struggle with thoughts of suicide.

The harder something is to talk about, the more likely it is that Travis is going to write about it. But he also enjoys writing about the other stuff...the drama and comedy of love and romantic relationships. Currently, he is obsessed with love and sensuality.

Often described as honest, vulnerable, and raw, Travis Montez has, early in his spoken word career, made a name for himself as a writer and audience-pleasing performer. His work has been featured in venues all over the world, including the American embassies of Spain and Senegal, the Nuyorican Poets Cafe, Brooklyn Cafe, New York University, and The Poetry Project at St. Mark's Church.

Travis has lent his talents to the Words to Comfort benefit for the World Trade Center Relief Fund, won the Black Gay Pride Slam in 2002, and is a regular feature in the House of Xavier's annual Glam Slam.

Travis Montez recently graduated from New York University's prestigious law program and is currently working as a lawyer.

good morning after

for Steven

[one]
i want to tell the children
to let him make you laugh first
before he touches you
or claims you
or marks you
opens you or makes you bleed
let him make you laugh
from the inside, out
the rest
will be more honest
and easy
...first kisses will come and go
you will slow dance
to the music of time
between touches
and breathe
...just let him make you laugh first
from the inside, out
the rest will fall
like rain in the summertime—
exactly where it belongs

[two]
it felt
like i'd said more than i had
perhaps
because i'd meant more
than the silly words
that danced from between my lips
i thought of him
on day two
as i got dressed
in the morning
wondering what i could wear
to make him notice me
and i thought
about my granny
and how she met my grandfather

when she wasn't looking
she was just humming a hymn and picking blackberries
and bumped into the rest of her life
and the truth was
i didn't want to make
him notice me
i just wanted him to see me
of his own free will
even if for just a moment in my life

[three]
the only other man
i've seen cook breakfast
is my father
and even he
only makes breakfast (for me)
to celebrate
baptisms
graduations
weddings
acceptable christian/middle-class things
that are easy to swallow
like his eggs
so as i watch this new man
dance at his stove
and ask me to unfold my life
with innocent-sounding questions
i am at home
but more honest
than i have ever been with my father
and i don't want to give him anything
that's too easy to swallow

[four]
i was kissing him
when the sun went down
and it was the first thing done
when i realized it was morning
and he was holding me/i was holding him on purpose
he dances around the room
as he gets ready for work
like he is alone
and i laugh on the inside
at how his body moves

i am already lining up the words
to explain this man and this day
to my friends
and it may take poetry
because they won't get it
without the imagery
"nothing happened" they will think
because he didn't fuck me
and there was no wet spot to speak of
but i will tell them
that my mind had multiple orgasms
when he
spoke about our people
and humanity
and intimacy
and *the simpsons*
and art and poetry
and he lit candles
and he played music
and he laughed at himself
and he smiled with his eyes
and i came
in all the most important ways
i will tell the children
that everything happened
and it was all still there the next morning
right where it belonged...

time piece

it is 2:53 a.m.
and i am 8 years old
and i wake up to the sound
of the first time
my father hit my mother
it is the hollow noise
of sound drowning reality
like screams caught in a paper bag
and it is only the first time
my father hits my mother
so he will explain himself:
"that's what you get for letting that boy
act like some damn sissie, embarrassing me
in front of my family"
he tells her
in that self-righteous, unapologetic way alcoholics do
just before he stumbles out the door
to chase manhood or avoid shame
and i cry myself back to sleep
and it is 3:47 a.m.
and i am 10 years old
and i wake up to hands that ain't mine
and a body that is not myself
finding me where i try to hide
covering my mouth
shoving NO back down my throat
burning into me
and i cannot remember what my laughter sounds like
because my favorite older cousin
has turned himself to judas
and i am to be betrayed and crucified
he has turned himself into a heavy shadow
that scratches at my soul
he has turned himself into a heavy whisper
i can never escape
reminding me that this is not the first time
reminding me of my childhood silence
bought with candy and his attention
convincing me that i like it
convincing me that They will hate me if i tell
that i am a faggot and that is the reason

180 bullets & butterflies

my father really left
convincing me that saturday mornings of shame
are the only love i will ever know
and he is all i have
it is 5:20 p.m.
i am 21 years old
and after a year
i say it
i tell him, "baby, i love you"
i tell him that he does not have to be afraid
i tell him that my soul has finally come out to play
but he
is a homophobic homosexual
and tells me that i am too gay
for him to be with
he tells me
that he needs someone
he can hang out with
on his block in queens
someone he can take home
and lie to his west indian mother about
because she is old-fashioned
and my feminine ways would offend her
plus, i do not like to play handball
"i can't see a thug like me,
being with someone like you"
he says
and the sun is going down
so i swallow myself and let him leave
without protest
silently wondering
if he is searching for manhood
or avoiding shame...
it is 8:14 p.m.
on a friday night
he is an hour late
and hasn't called
it is raining
and i cannot see
the williamsburg bridge from my window
and the only reason i chose this apartment
was for the view at night
and since i am thinking about bridges and choices
i wonder how much more of my life

will be spent
choosing to watch clocks and count minutes
waiting for phone calls that will not come
waiting for apologies that will not come
as though my forgiveness is not worthy
as though i am not worthy
and since i am thinking of worthiness and redemption
i contemplate trying to fly from my window
and meeting concrete sidewalks
to separate what i know is beautiful on the inside
from the heavy, scarred cage that is my outside
freeing myself of this skin i have outgrown
and since i am thinking of black skin and men
i consider hating black men again
but instead i call my mother
and listen to her tell me about my first step
and how i learned to spell at three
and how my grandmother
who took care of rich white babies just to feed her own
would read to me from the bible like it was my family tree
and said i would grow up to be something special
and this leaves my heart no room
for hate or suicide
and i cry myself to sleep
feeling saved

over me

he wrote
number one gay nigger
across his son's skull
because he thought
that was my name
he wrote
number one gay nigger
across his son's skull
because he thought
that was my name
and he wrote
my name
across his son's skull
because
i loved him
number one gay nigger
and i loved the son
when the father
couldn't stand
black americans or faggots
couldn't stand black americans
with their loud music
their tacky gold chains
their disrespectful baggy pants
and he wasn't about to let his son
be no faggot
over no
number one gay nigger
like me
see
he had traded
one star for fifty
just so his son
could be a man
and
a number one gay nigger
would ruin that dream,
would make that move
from one island with palm trees
to another island with skyscrapers
useless

and he couldn't stand
black americans or faggots
couldn't stand black americans
or their music
that crying-wailing-dying black people music
that sounded like sin
he couldn't stand their music
except for that one song
that:
over time
i've been building my castle of love
just for two
although you
never knew
you were my reason
he liked that one song
about love and trying
about losing and finding
because he thought
it was about him
but at the end of the day
he still wrote
number one gay nigger
across his son's skull
just to keep him
from saying my name
and the ironic thing
is just like that song,
over heart
i had painfully turned every stone
just to find
that sometimes
fathers love leviticus
more than they love their own sons
like isaac on the altar
like jesus on the cross
sons stand forsaken
bleeding for sins
they can't name
number one gay nigger
and
he sacrificed his son
just so
he wouldn't love

no
number one gay nigger
no faggot black american
with music in the dark
no
number one gay nigger
like me
over dreams
i thought things
would be easy
believing stevie
when he said
true love just needs a chance
but we never had a chance
because one sunday morning
while the son was sleeping
the father was thinking
about all the nasty things
we must've been doing
the night before
one sunday morning
while the son was sleeping
the father was thinking
about all the places
i must have touched his son
with my dirty nigga-faggot hands
and all his dreams
seemed deferred
he had cashed in
one star for fifty
just so his son could be a man,
he traded islands
he traded puerto rico for manhattan
he traded islands and sand castles
for el barrio and manhood
but his son
wouldn't be a man
if i could touch him
like that
in the dark
if i could touch him
with my music
if i could touch him
with my heart

so, one sunday morning
while the son was sleeping
the father took his breath away
he took that life away
and when the father was done
there was no son
only a body torn to pieces
flesh removed from bone
because he had been looking
for the little thing
that made his son a faggot
and when he could not find it
and there was only the skull
when there was nothing left but the skull
he wrote his reason across it,
he addressed it to me,
he wrote
he scratched
he carved
number one gay nigger
across his son's skull
because he thought
that was my name
he killed his son
over sex with a man
over sex with a
number one gay nigger
he killed his son
over islands traded
over sand castles given away
over what people might say
over machismo bullshit
he killed his son
over time
over love
over a number one gay nigger
over me

nothing new under the sun

1. Tennessee/5:53 p.m.

the sun sets here
like a lover returning to bed
hands following light
to places
still warm and soft
from this morning's rise
ushering in silence and sleep
with breathtaking kisses
through sycamore trees
in these moments
just before night
everything seems more alive
even as the sun goes
in small, beautiful deaths
of color and time
as the day lays herself down
and sighs her meaning
behind mountains
and rivers
that run into the distance
blue is the first to go
the sky becomes pale
yielding to the undone color of clouds
the sun then gives up her red and orange
bleeds to pink
and purple dances
from one horizon to the other
planting stars in her wake
hoping they will grow
as my lover tennessee sun sleeps
and moon is born

2. Brooklyn/4:57 p.m.

you can watch
from rooftops
and make a wish
but you have to wish real hard
so it will reach

over brownstones and project towers
and from here
it would be easy
to believe
she is the last thing left
that god has made
you would love her
from brooklyn
if you had the time
to stand on rooftops
and watch her
at the end of the day
because that's what it means:
today is done
with all you have won or lost
today is memory
empty hands
forgiveness and mercy
today is done
clenched fists
and holding on
cannot change that
not now, not up here
on a rooftop in brooklyn
as you watch her go down over the city
and night comes
from behind you...
know that tomorrow she will be back
(she rises over brooklyn)
to let you do it better/harder/sooner/or later
than you did it before
with open/empty hands
and memory

3. Tennessee/Granddaddy's House

i have always been here
where my grandfather's cornfields
and my granny's peach trees
used to be
i have always been here
on this land
bought with colored peoples' money
saved from cleaning white peoples' churches

and raising white peoples' kids
i have always been here
where my mama was a little girl
and i have always played in this grass
ridden my bike on these dirt roads
climbed these trees to their very tops
and imagined a kingdom
of countrysides and creeks
i have always been here
in a place we've called our own
and places like this are rare
places where the children
of sharecroppers and mammies
can imagine kingdoms
and play beyond the reach
of police and street corners
and ghosts of "whites only" signs
and church bombings
these rare places
where we can dream
and climb and fall and get back up
and chase cousins and rabbits
watch birds fly over us
and ponder the meaning
of butterflies and bee stings
discover honeysuckle
and tree sap
eat the fruit our grandmothers planted
where our laughter will chorus
with the dreams of our parents
on land where we truly belong...

4. Brooklyn/Sunset Park

from the third floor
of a brownstone
i dream new things
my apartment is in the home
of a Puerto Rican mother
who reminds me of my own
because she too comes from fruit trees
and candor and music
and nights spent dancing
under moons she could name

so i live here in brooklyn
among people who remind me
of my grandfather's front yard
and what i want the whole world to be
hardworking people
still alive enough to dream
and plant their children next to hope
and the passion of sunsets
i have always been here
i will always be here
dreaming of kingdoms
of freedom
where we truly belong

pray for rain

this poem is part Me
because on a tuesday in september
there are angels burning in the sky
and I wonder if god is trying to write my name
I can smell the smoke from where I stand
and see people fleeing the towers
from windows like robins with no wings
trading one death for another
my heart hears their screams
and always will
on a tuesday in september
words are hummingbirds
no longer in my mouth
babel has fallen
people on broadway are quoting nostradamus
and I am running to collect everything that I love
this poem is part Brooklyn
because locked behind brownstone doors
she remembers the last time this happened
after oklahoma
before the devil had a white man's name
there were gunshots through store windows
and hate graffiti on mosque walls
she is afraid to let her son go to school
she is afraid that american helplessness
will find its way into his skull
or chase him into the streets
and tear him to pieces
though he has never seen afghanistan
and only knows his homeland
from phone calls and legends
she is afraid that they will tear him apart
because he is here and they are afraid
and there is nothing else that they can do
this poem is part Love
because busy signals are keeping us apart
and I think of all the times
I have hated him
because I love him so much
he is my best friend
and at 9:05 on a tuesday

he is supposed to be working
on wall street
at a job that he has no passion for
and because I know him so well
part of me knows that he is okay
because he would have gotten up late
tired from being at the gym last night
but I am worried
because his late is an if
not a certainty
and there are busy signals
where his voice should be
this poem is part American
because I am afraid
I keep dreaming of fire and burning flesh
as bodies are found and named
as I see my friends evacuate homes and places of work
as I see the hopeful carrying pictures
of missing loved ones like crosses
red, white, and blue have a whole new meaning
part of my humanity is missing
and I am afraid that I will never get it back
and this poem is part Me again
because there is guilt
that I hold so much love in my hands
and it is all still there
when so many others are shattered from loss
because there is joy
that my refrain has become I am still alive
I am still alive...

revolution of bottoms

this poem is about my ass
this poem is about men who have sex to colonize
and compromise
what has taken a lifetime to set free
because my humanity
cannot be sodomized or ripped from parted thighs
this poem is about my ass
that has a name that sounds nothing like pussy
because I have a name that sounds nothing like bitch
because good sex is freedom
and because I want to be free
this poem is about virginity
lost to a homophobic cousin
and the dozen nameless faces who've taken his place
but I have taken my inner space back
from black boys with something to prove
and latin kings with baby's mama tattoos
this poem is about my ass
and high school boys with clumsy hands
this poem is about my ass
and the condoms that broke
this poem is about my ass
and the times I pretended it didn't hurt just to make him happy
this poem is about my ass
and letting him call me his wife just so he could be a man
this poem is about my ass
and learning that I don't have to choose between being sexy
        and being smart
this poem is about my ass
and the pornographic fiction that I've let define me
this poem is about my ass
this poem is about freedom
this poem is about real love
that doesn't hurt when made carefully
this poem is because some fool thinks he's the best sex I've ever had
when he's just the sex I'm having right now
this poem is because he will never have me again
this poem is because people take the label Bottom too literally
this poem is because labels irritate my ass' skin
this poem is because my ass has a name that sounds nothing like pussy
this poem is about taking date but not taking shit

this poem is about my ass
this poem is about Whose is it?
this poem is because it's mine

a real love poem

[one]
you send him love poems
that you didn't write
to express emotions
you don't really feel
and your betrayal of me/is useless
because i am all the poet he will ever need
you try to read between lines
that were never written for you
but miss the meaning of my presence:
the fact that i am here
means that you can't be here
can you hear me getting to know him?
can you hear me
excited about holding hands
and walks in the village
hear him making me breakfast for lunch
just because breakfast is my favorite meal
hear him call me his soft, sweet, beautiful precious
hear him make me laugh
from the inside out
can you hear all these things
without regretting my happiness
you send him love poems
that you've never fully read or understood
by poets you can't even pronounce
to express thoughts you don't even think
and your actions are silly to me
because i am all the poet he will ever need
and understand
that this is not
a gum-popping
neck-rolling
oh-no-you-didn't-
try-to-take-my-man poem
because i have learned that men
cannot be taken or possessed
if you can "steal" him from my life
with your plagiarized ego-dramas
then he was never really mine
no. the poet is not threatened

only tired
of raising you, brotha
in the places your parents
never thought to look
i don't want to try and find you anymore, brotha
because you don't want a friend
you only want
someone to be lonely with
and you regret my happiness
like it was a mistake you made

[two]
love poems
do not happen
accidentally
they cannot be cut nor pasted
not sampled, looped,
nor taken out of context
they are specific and unique
like fingerprints
and first kisses
love poems are real
and imperfect
they happen when you are not looking
when you think no one is watching
love poems are lived
then written
on subway rides home from first dates
or while your clothes still smell like him
or at work when you can't concentrate
even though your project is an hour late
you can't do anything until you have to find
the right combination of words and self
to describe an orgasm
that felt like sunshine and church and etta james and
a reason to record life
love poems
do not happen accidentally
they are real and imperfect
and unconditional

[three]
but you would not know these things
because you are not a poet

you are not me
you are definitely not all the poet he will ever need

[four]
we dance to tweet's slow songs
(track 2 makes him kiss me)
and press our bodies together
in candlelight
until a universe
is created between us
and the rules of eden are rewritten across our backs
he prays my name
and i answer his prayers
because i want him here
in my own image
in the beginning
i gave him my words
to keep
among his precious things
he wears them now
like diamonds
and quotes them like scripture
i am all the poet he will ever need

[five]
wounded in the house of a friend
i have nothing left to plant
or feed you
keep these words
among your precious things
let them be real and imperfect lived
after bridges are burned and the lonely comes
let it be all the poem you will ever need

Staceyann Chin

staceyann chin

Staceyann Chin is a full-time artist.

A resident of New York City and a Jamaican national, she has been an "out poet and political activist" since '98.

In 1998, Staceyann Chin was the winner of the Lambda Poetry Slam and the Slam This! competition.

In 1999, she was the winner of the Chicago People of Color Slam; first runner-up in the Outwrite Poetry Slam; a finalist in the Nuyorican Grand Slam; and the winner of *WORD*, the first slam for television. That same year, Staceyann took the American Amazon Slam title in Aarhus, Denmark, and graced the cover of the national newspaper, *The Politiken*, as well as the controversial and spicy *Ekstra Bladet*.

In 2000, she was the winner of another Slam This! and her first one-woman show, *Hands Afire*, ran for ten weeks at the Bleecker Theater.

In 2001, the same Off-Broadway theater welcomed her second one-woman show, *Unspeakable Things*, before she took it to Copenhagen for a week-long run. Also that year, the film *Staceyann Chin* was released in Danish theaters and eventually aired on Danish National Television.

In 2002, Staceyann was nominated for the Rolex Mentor and Protégé Art Initiative, where she was considered as a possible protégé for Toni Morrison.

The year 2003 brought a remarkably successful whirlwind tour of South Africa: Cape Town, Durban, Johannesburg, and a quick visit to Soweto. Staceyann was asked to be the first poet commissioned to write and perform a piece with the prestigious Dance Africa Chicago.

Staceyann Chin has appeared on *60 Minutes*, the Peabody Award–winning HBO series, *Russell Simmons presents Def Poetry*, and

PBS's Emmy-nominated newsmagazine, *In the Life*. She has also co-written and performed as one of the original cast members of the groundbreaking and critically acclaimed, Tony Award–winning *Russell Simmons Def Poetry Jam on Broadway*.

Staceyann's work has appeared in the *New York Times*, the *Washington Post*, and the *Pittsburgh Daily*. Her poetry can also be found in her first chapbook, *Wildcat Woman*, and the one she now carries on her back, *Stories Surrounding My Coming*, and numerous anthologies, including *Skyscrapers, Taxis and Tampons, Poetry Slam, Role Call*, and *Cultural Studies: Critical Methodologies*. She can also be heard on the CD, *5 Past 13 – a little bit LOUDER: Volume 1*.

Between the Lines, a film that explores the notion of being Asian and woman and writer, is the latest documentary to feature Staceyann Chin.

From the rousing cheers of the Nuyorican Poets Cafe to her one-woman shows Off-Broadway to poetry workshops in Denmark and London to her stints on television and Broadway, Staceyann credits the long list of "things she has done" to her grandmother's hardworking history and the pain of her mother's absence. Still fighting for time to finish all the other projects she has begun, Staceyann Chin is desperately trying to create some room to travel to see her sister and simply to breathe.

on jumping off ledges
of impossibilities

You be up
in my gut like intestines
twisting away at my insides
like a blade
you be difficult to fade
like a discordant song composed to go higher
when it's ending
I play you incessant
over and over
to remind me
that we never began anything
really
never began
nothing

Odd how I remember make-believe notes about you
                minor keys in succession
                of she wants me
                she wants me not
                it sure is crazy how I already fancy myself in love
                with the sound of you coming from Omaha
or Idaho
                Michigan is the one place you made time for me
a bathroom in Frisco
is all I have
because I don't want to demand too much of you
don't want the slender bridge that connects us
to break because I had to show my lack
of home training
or patience
or the vision
to see that you were struggling with the decision
to see me before I dash off to Europe
or maybe because your woman wouldn't let you
go
all the way across the world
to see some strange woman read sonnets in Scotland

Denmark would be

200 bullets & butterflies

the love song you might write
about us
        two black girls on a ferry from
        Copenhagen to Malmo
we could circumvent fate
with the canal surrounding the city with almost no poverty
        wouldn't we be living pretty off the fat
of someone else's land

I want to know
what the small of my back
would feel like with your hand holding it
in Ireland

I want you to want me like you want
her to change
I want the freedom to write you like you want her to paint
        beautiful
and without hesitation
        I am lobbying
        for whole weekends in Washington
        to fuck you
        relentless in Berlin
and it not be a sin in Atlanta

The more practical parts of me recommend
resignation from this post of almost
lover
only sort of emotional
nearly-but-not-quite-fucking-you-friend

this cannot end well

so I have quietly decided to construct this
maybe-ultimatum-perhaps-even-final-farewell
before I find myself
three flights up on a broken fire escape
threatening to jump
or push you
over some ill-conceived ledge of impossibility

lesbian chasing straight

I told her
I liked the way she made that pink push-up bra look
intellectual—and she laughed
beautiful/confident/deadly
turned her color-treated blow-dried
bone-straight just-curled arrogance the other way and roared

I almost told her,
       "if you didn't have that perm you'd be perfect"
        —only a scorned woman's opinion
it hangs on the uncertain balance of her laughter
still
I wanted to go after her—beg her to sit with me awhile
lipstick that smile to the tip of my pen
maybe then she would allow for my fingers
constructing the perfect poem on the hollows of her elbows
the line of her neck made me want to paint her
brush tattooing words up the inside of her ankle
tongue caressing metered shadows under her knees
how I wanted to please that woman
with the things I have learned to do to a body

But straight girls require more than the catchy lesbian line
they need more than the average stitch
in these times of weak-kneed freedoms
the bi-curious require a puss' whole nine lives
as they move in for the kill
it is a skill they perfect in the practice of rejection

The slow grind of her heels sank into my wilting desire
she spun away perfume and attitude swirling
the lines in my head twirling to the lift of her skirt
       a boy I kissed once
       maybe twice
       told me that straight girls require work and study
and a different kind of program
       I had to stop to remind myself
of the curriculum for lesbian chasing straight
       rule # 1. You have to be platonic first
means you are nothing more than a friend
—you cannot bend that rule for the first three months

everything must be the same as you began
until she adjusts
the plan is really to wait until there is a crack
in the lack of respect her boyfriend has for her
you must reinforce how she deserves *so* much better
          you must have a vision
be ready to make quick decisions in the interest of her time
—offer her your money
the comfort of your bed
save the bold statement of intent for when she is lying there
bent double with the need to be held
cradle her
tell her she is beautiful in the least objective language of your lust
stroke her
go gently toward her light spaces
kiss her hands—resist the urge to ask her to go down on all fours
drink beer from a brown bottle
or recite 20th-Century prose while she is being entered
          do not insist on the norm of versatility right away

do expect her to become that run-of-the-mill dyke
with the 11 and a ½ plus one flesh-colored dildos
the two essays on middle-American homophobia
three multispeed vibrators
each with converters for Northern Europe
England and Australia—all rechargeable
avoid talk of the fluorescent butt plug right away
wait until you have had her
glowing in the stairwell with the lights turned on
her belly on your back
her back to the ground
          there will be time enough to show her how
lesbian sex has a way of being outrageous
what with the bedposts and those handcuffs
with the fur in the middle
wet spots and warm rags applied between giggles

Straight girls are unable to swallow the whole syllabus in the first class
so I resisted the urge to go after her
silenced the arguments developing in my head
I never said another word to her
          but between you and me
all that perfume and arrogance aside
I could have taught her a thing or two

she could have learned something new
about gender-bending and multiple orgasms
maybe she could have taught me things about the way I've been coming
to terms with my own sexuality
but straight girls are often unwilling to make that slide
now and then one might even dip her hand all the way in
but only to test the tide
and most of us dykes enjoy the time of day they choose to give us
only in private do we confess that straight girls require too much effort
and stitches in groups larger than the accepted nine
and on that afternoon in question
I could neither afford the insults, the expense, nor the time

trini girl: for lynne

Trini girl
with you grandmother silence
twisted tight into the roots of your copper locks
      the follicle a shade darker than the tips
      wish you could tell me
exactly where the color hurts
      when the great light of mornings
      dark showers and see-through
      tears are not enough to hold you
together
      let me hold you
      sometimes
      let us
      mourn the loss of some lover or other
together
      be dazzling beyond the lyric of rhymes we turn
like tricks to convince each other
      we are surviving

      I know you are surviving

      I recognize the Toni gleam
in the slow pivot of emotion you carry in your mother's
mother's   indifference
spine ramrod   straight
backbone   upright and unending
body perfect   between   us

      I am grateful for the parallax
      of wet in your eye

my own vision is frequently   obscured
tears/island love song/   the rescue/the constant
      the cooing   "hush girl—   everything go be alright"
too oftenyou pull away   too fast
      but when you know my shoulders
have stopped   the heaving   the sloping
the need for things I have not learnt to say

I wish you would stay longer
      sometimes

wish I could ask how the night went
or how you swallow the sorrow   alone
the clear uncertain saliva   rushing
off your back

How do you stand the lack of warm
in your bed
              your white sheets stained
only with the scent of memory

wish I could ask you the questions
we seem to raise
              only in metaphors

But I have long learned to hold you
              close with clever knots of dyed
              hair tied into the known performance

I have accepted your grandmother's silence

I have learned to recognize the gleam
              in the tiny flash of light that no longer haunts me
              it just makes me want to hold you
              more now
              because I know how you cry

thesis on love

I've bought the bloody myth

swallowed that sucker
hairy legs and all
crawled careless into bed with a fantasy
and now I'm hopping antsy with expectation

      having drawn these crooked lines
in what looked to me like sand
my uncertain frame stands
hooked
on what I have been promised by the TV
by that saccharine ache Anita Baker
moans from a mass-produced CD

The game of happily ever after in love
is a cruel farce
      the lonely wish of a gullible asshole
who somebody done told
a whole lot of silly lies to
love is nothing
but the by-product of a teenager
wagering hormonal changes
against the smell of his own diluted sperm
spilling innocent into his awkward palm

Love is the alms
given to the poor to divert
focus from the difference
between the shacks that teachers live in
in Brooklyn
and the mansions that senators fuck young interns in
in Washington, DC

I am just about ready to give up
on man
woman
dog and tree
the whole romantic tic is hogwash

The idiots

who look like they might still be in love
have only been together
for three weeks
and those lucky enough to have lasted more than a year
are rapidly shifting gears
towards chopping the shared
now-dysfunctional cat
in two equal parts
so they can cart the rest of their shit
to the new apartment
they cannot afford by themselves

I am tired of searching for Ms. Right
       always something wrong
       with the one girl who likes me
too smart
too skinny
too much of a ninny
too short/too tall
too-much-of-a-mall-girl for my liking
too free/too taken/too I'm sorry I was mistaken
in my initial assessment of your sexuality
       sometimes
       I think I hang my hat too high
       for my own arms to reach them
which brings me back
to my original hypothesis
of love being somewhat like the perfect orgasm
       the trip there
is infinitely better than the letdown
of having already experienced it

       After the first
actualization of intercourse
there's no up to go from there
what is one to do with the sticky wet
of saliva
and vaginal fluid
and sweat
not drying fast enough
in the center of a lumpy futon
you are desperately trying to fall asleep in

Love
as I have understood it
is primarily disappointment
and hard work and very little return
so now I'm canvassing for volunteers
to go tar the cupid who conjured
the stupid concept
feather the fucker and leave the body to burn

christmas

It is the end of an era
holy
family
Trinity
the air is expectant with my mother's arrival
miracle on Beach 29th Street
my mother's slender frame fills the door in my house

It is the season of perpetual cheer
Christmas and my family is here
finally things are as they should be
and naturally there is a tree
the presents jumbled beneath the glitter of rainbow wishes
everything is perfect on the surface
the smiles are not cracking yet
for now we have agreed to tiptoe round the fallen needles
that litter the newly carpeted floor
my mother has not called me a whore yet
she has not refused to meet my lover yet
Santa is still on his way
two days after her arrival and my sister is still laughing
shrill as only children do
there is light mention of my brother
no talk of how he hates his mother more than I ever will

Everything is as it should be
on the surface
I am not choking on the wishbone of a dream come horribly true

We have not argued
yet
I have not admitted to anyone that I do not want her in my home
        the family I have chosen is wary of her wigged smile
        her flawed grammar the quilted stories she constructs for
        anyone who will
listen
she insists she did no wrong in leaving me when she did
look around you
everything turned out as it should
could you have done better than being the writer
the rape-child

confessing the details of her mother's life
my child is also a lesbian who does nothing with her hair

                    She is as disappointed
                    as I am unable to admit
I am ashamed of my mother's awkward gait
her wild eyes
I do not understand why she is not the parent I waited for
I wanted her to be magnificent
she was supposed to come and save me
but I cannot even write while that woman is in my room
I cannot make love while she is in my bed
cannot read what she is thinking when she looks at me with those eyes
when speaks to me only through my sister
my expectations were unrealistic my friends say
the television lies to the Thanksgiving public
blood ties do not tighten during the holiday
New Year's is not the day
to introduce your gay husband to your homophobic estranged mother

I should have known her
before she left the second man who wronged her
before my father
my brother's father
my sister's German father is a foreign name my sister carries
        without pride
my mother rides her for being his child
her hair must never be wild
she must be the perfect almost-white child
she must learn to win the battles her mother never had the chance
        to fight
it is her birthright
my failure

It is not my job to save her from the woman whose disapproval is
        a given
we never have to ask for the reasons we lack so much of what she
        would prefer
our backs are never straight enough for her
and I am ashamed of her insanity
her ability to right away kill the laughter in a room
her arrival is a tomb from which my poems do not come readily
my fingers are numb from the effort of trying
while she sleeps uncertain between my blue sheets

staceyann chin 211

I lie awake and she plans how best to turn the blade to her advantage
        if my mother becomes frightened enough
        I might never see my sister again
the pen sinks into my barren palm
I cannot close my fist without cutting someone
I am afraid it might be me

Everything is as it should be
        on the surface the mother
the lesbian/the child/the absent brother
beneath the green glitter the fallen needles
burrow, darken as we skirt around each other

audre lorde

for Audre and the women who walked through History alongside her

I am sorry you had to go
before I came running to your America

A place of capitalistic contradictions
it is still safer than my Jamaica
for a woman like me
a woman like you
loud
black lover of black men
and women you gave birth to two children
and a generation of screamers

Your essays and your poems
presented to the world in protest against
our own internalized racism and homophobia defined
new worlds for old women who could not see themselves as beautiful
your pen opened a path for others like me
to find a way into our own names

Can you see the colors from where you are, Audre?

Bright rainbows blazing in every major city of the modern world
summer parades grin pink triangles
red ribbons resting easy on the scarred chests of sisters
still battling breast cancer

your journals remain
as testimony
to the many faces of that struggle

Your fury fuels my own fire
flickering weak on those nights when I have to come out
onstage to a new crowd

Those nights I imagine your hands holding my rage
against all the new names I have learned to call myself
bitch and ho and nothing — we are still property —
the Mistress of Mr. So-and-So
we are still more valuable as young as pretty —

I am afraid for the gravity of what remains to be done

We have come the proverbial long way
but only so far—the war continues against poverty in black
    neighborhoods
        they still have not paid us back for injuries incurred
traveling through the middle passage
women still make only 67 percent of what the average man takes home
for doing the same job
they are now killing more of us in their jails
nailing our sons to the cross of a white religion
and I still cannot marry a woman I love
unless I fucking move to Scandinavia

All this I rail in accordance with the women
who came before me
before you as Sojourners speaking
Truth; as Harriet Tubmans, and Virginia Woolfs
I call on the courage of those who knew you well
Barbara Smith, Pat Parker, Sonia Sanchez
I call on you
woman whose words I have come to know too well
help me give these new millennia motherfuckers hell
send me a signal
find a way to let me know
that invoking the memory of the fighters who came before us
is more than enough to take us through all the places we still
    have to go